Brady v. Maryland Material in the United States District Courts: Rules, Orders, and Policies

*Report to the
Advisory Committee on Criminal Rules
of the Judicial Conference of the United States*

Federal Judicial Center
May 31, 2007

Brady v. Maryland Material
in the United States District Courts:
Rules, Orders, and Policies

*Report to the
Advisory Committee on Criminal Rules
of the Judicial Conference of the United States*

Laural Hooper and Shelia Thorpe

Federal Judicial Center

May 31, 2007

This report was undertaken in furtherance of the Federal Judicial Center's statutory mission to conduct and stimulate research and development for the improvement of judicial administration. The views expressed are those of the authors and not necessarily those of the Federal Judicial Center.

Contents

I. Introduction, 1
   A. Background: *Brady*, Rule 16, and Rule 11, 2
      1. Brady v. Maryland, 2
      2. Federal Rule of Criminal Procedure 16, 4
      3. Federal Rule of Criminal Procedure 11, 5
      4. American College of Trial Lawyers' proposal, 6
      5. Department of Justice's response to the ACTL's proposal, 6
      6. Summary of Advisory Committee's and Department of Justice's work on amending Rule 16, 6
   B. Summary of Findings, 7

II. U.S. District Court Rules and Policies Addressing *Brady* Material, 9
   A. Research Methods, 9
   B. Governing Rules, Orders, and Procedures, 10
   C. Definition of *Brady* Material, 10
      1. Evidence favorable to the defendant, 12
      2. Exculpatory evidence or exculpatory material, 12
      3. *Brady* material generally, 14
   D. Disclosure Requirements, 14
      1. Time requirements for disclosure, 15
      2. Duration of disclosure requirements, 17
   E. Due Diligence Requirements, 18
   F. Sanctions for Noncompliance with *Brady* Obligations, 19
   G. Declination Procedures, 20

Appendix A: Proposed Rule 16 Amendment and Committee Note, 23

Appendix B: Compendium of U.S. District Court Material Addressing *Brady* Material, 25

Appendix C: Sample of Individual Judge Orders Addressing *Brady* Disclosures, 39

Appendix D: *U.S. Attorney's Manual*, Section 9-5.000, Issues Related to Trials and Other Court Proceedings, 43

Appendix E: State Court Policies for the Treatment of *Brady* Material, 49

I. Introduction

In April 2007, the Judicial Conference Advisory Committee on Criminal Rules asked the Federal Judicial Center to update its 2004 report on local rules of the U.S. district courts, state laws, and state court rules that address the disclosure principles contained in *Brady v. Maryland*.[1] *Brady* requires that prosecutors fully disclose to the accused all exculpatory evidence in the prosecutors' possession. Subsequent Supreme Court decisions have elaborated the *Brady* obligations to include the duty to disclose (1) impeachment evidence,[2] (2) favorable evidence in the absence of a request by the accused,[3] and (3) "favorable evidence known to the others acting on the government's behalf in the case including the police."[4]

When it requested the 2004 report, the committee's interest was in learning whether federal district courts and state courts have adopted any formal rules or standards that provide prosecutors with specific guidance on discharging their *Brady* obligations. Specifically, the committee wanted to know whether the U.S. district and state courts' relevant authorities (1) codify the *Brady* rule, (2) set specific deadlines for when *Brady* material must be disclosed, or (3) require *Brady* material to be disclosed automatically or only on request. In addition, the Center sought information regarding policies in two areas: (1) due diligence obligations of the government to locate and disclose *Brady* material favorable to the defendant, and (2) sanctions for the government's failure to comply specifically with *Brady* disclosure obligations. That research resulted in a report titled *Treatment of Brady v. Maryland Material in United States District and State Courts' Rules, Orders, and Policies*.

This 2007 report has two sections and five appendices. Section I presents a general introduction to the report, along with a summary of our findings. Section II describes the federal district court local rules, orders, and policies that address *Brady* material. Appendix A contains the committee's proposed amendment to Rule 16. Appendix B is a compendium of federal material that served as the basis for this report. Appendix C provides examples of individual judge orders addressing *Brady* disclosures. Appendix D contains the *U.S. Attorney's Manual*, section 9-5.000, *Issues Related to Trials and Other Court Proceedings*, which covers the Department of Justice's policy regarding disclosure of exculpatory and im-

---

1. 373 U.S. 83 (1963).
2. Giglio v. United States, 405 U.S. 150, 153–54 (1972).
3. United States v. Agurs, 427 U.S. 97, 107 (1976).
4. Kyles v. Whitley, 514 U.S. 419, 437 (1995).

peachment information. Appendix E includes the state court portion of the 2004 *Brady* report. It has not been updated.

A. Background: *Brady*, Rule 16, and Rule 11

1. *Brady v. Maryland*

In *Brady v. Maryland*, the Supreme Court held "that the suppression by the prosecution of evidence favorable to an accused upon request violates due process where the evidence is material either to guilt or punishment, irrespective of the good faith or bad faith of the prosecution."[5] Subsequent Supreme Court decisions have held that the government has a constitutionally mandated, affirmative duty to disclose exculpatory evidence to the defendant to help ensure the defendant's right to a fair trial under the Fifth and Fourteenth Amendments' Due Process Clauses.[6] The Court cited as justification for the disclosure obligation of prosecutors "the special role played by the American prosecutor in the search for truth in criminal trials."[7] The prosecutor serves as "'the representative . . . of a sovereignty . . . whose interest . . . in a criminal prosecution is not that it shall win a case, but that justice shall be done.'"[8]

The *Brady* decision did not define what types of evidence are considered "material" to guilt or punishment, but other decisions have attempted to do so. For example, the standard of "materiality" for undisclosed evidence that would constitute a *Brady* violation has evolved over time from "if the omitted evidence creates a reasonable doubt that did not otherwise exist,"[9] to "if there is a reasonable probability that, had the evidence been disclosed to the defense, the result of the proceeding would have been different,"[10] to "whether in [the undisclosed evidence's] absence [the defendant] received a fair trial, understood as a trial resulting in a verdict worthy of confidence,"[11] to the current standard: "when prejudice to the accused ensues . . . [and where] the nondisclosure [is] so serious that there

---

5. *Brady*, 373 U.S. at 87.
6. *See* United States v. Bagley, 473 U.S. 667, 675 (1985) ("The *Brady* rule is based on the requirement of due process. Its purpose is not to displace the adversary system as the primary means by which truth is uncovered, but to ensure that a miscarriage of justice does not occur.").
7. Strickler v. Greene, 527 U.S. 263, 281 (1999).
8. Kyles v. Whitley, 514 U.S. 419, 439 (1995) (quoting Berger v. United States, 295 U.S. 78, 88 (1935)).
9. United States v. Agurs, 427 U.S. 97, 112 (1976).
10. *Bagley*, 473 U.S. at 682.
11. *Kyles*, 514 U.S. at 434.

is a reasonable probability that the suppressed evidence would have produced a different verdict."[12]

Over the last few years, a number of articles have been written regarding prosecutorial obligations and discretion pursuant to *Brady*.[13] Those articles highlight some of the issues that continue to be raised and debated in the legal community. (Please note that the articles cited are not intended to serve as a comprehensive review of the literature on this issue.)

One author investigated the "dissonance between *Brady*'s grand expectation to civilize U.S. criminal justice and the grim reality of its largely unfilled promise."[14] Further, the author proffers that the lack of specific local court rules imposing obligations on prosecutors impedes compliance.[15] Others argue that current disciplinary mechanisms provide little remedy.[16]

---

12. *Strickler*, 527 U.S. at 281–82.

13. Stephanos Bibas, *The Story of Brady v. Maryland: From Adversarial Gameship Toward the Search for Innocence?*, U. Pa. L. Sch., Working Paper No. 81 (2005) (http://lsr.nellco.org/upenn/wps/papers/81); Elizabeth Napier Dewar, *A Fair Trial Remedy for Brady Violations*, 115 Yale L.J. 1450 (2006); Bennett L. Gershman, *Reflections on Brady v. Maryland*, 47 S. Tex. L. Rev. 685 (2005–2006); Peter A. Joy, *The Relationship Between Prosecutorial Misconduct and Wrongful Convictions: Shaping Remedies for a Broken System*, 2006 Wis. L. Rev. 399 (2006); John B. Mitchell, *Evaluating Brady Error Using Narrative Theory: A Proposal for Reform*, 53 Drake L. Rev. 599 (2005); Mark D. Villaverde, *Structuring the Prosecutor's Duty to Search the Intelligence Community for Brady Material*, 88 Cornell L. Rev. 1471 (2003).

14. Gershman, *supra* note 13, at 686. *See also* Scott E. Sundby, *Superheroes and Constitutional Mirages: The Take of Brady v. Maryland*, 33 McGeorge L. Rev. 643, 658 (2002) (positing that "*Brady*'s doctrinal limitations as a pre-trial discovery mechanism are magnified by the realities of criminal practice").

15. Gershman, *supra* note 13, at 726 (citing United States v. Mannarino, 850 F. Supp. 57, 59, 71 (D. Mass. 1994) (finding that prosecutors had consistently, for many years, shown an "obdurate indifference to . . . disclosure responsibilities," prompting the district to adopt an extensive discovery rule)).

16. Peter Joy, *The Relationship Between Prosecutorial Misconduct and Wrongful Convictions: Shaping Remedies for a Broken System*, Wis. L. Rev. 399, 400 (2006) (suggesting "prosecutorial misconduct is largely the result of three institutional conditions: vague ethics rules that provide ambiguous guidance to prosecutors; vast discretionary authority with little or no transparency; and inadequate remedies for prosecutorial misconduct, which create perverse incentives for prosecutors to engage in, rather than refrain from, prosecutorial misconduct"); Joseph R. Weeks, *No Wrong Without a Remedy: The Effective Enforcement of the Duty of Prosecutors to Disclose Exculpatory Evidence*, 22 Okla. City U. L. Rev. 833, 898 (1997) (concluding that most disciplinary processes are almost completely ineffective against prosecutors); Ellen Yaroshefsky, *Wrongful Convictions: It Is Time to Take Prosecution Discipline Seriously*, 8 D.C. L. Rev. 275, 289–91 (2004) (exploring the efficacy of prosecutors' manuals, the Office of Professional Responsibility, and bar disciplinary committees).

Lastly, one author has proposed an innovative remedy for criminal defendants when the government fails to fulfill its constitutional obligation to disclose favorable evidence.[17]

2. *Federal Rule of Criminal Procedure 16*

Federal Rule of Criminal Procedure 16 governs discovery and inspection of evidence in federal criminal cases. The Notes of the Advisory Committee to the 1974 Amendments expressly said that in revising Rule 16 "to give greater discovery to both the prosecution and the defense," the committee had "decided not to codify the *Brady* Rule."[18] However, the committee explained, "the requirement that the government disclose documents and tangible objects 'material to the preparation of his defense' underscores the importance of disclosure of evidence favorable to the defendant."[19]

Rule 16 entitles the defendant to receive, upon request, the following information:

- statements made by the defendant;
- the defendant's prior criminal record;
- documents and tangible objects within the government's possession that "are material to the preparation of the defendant's defense or are intended for use by the government as evidence in chief at the trial, or were obtained from or belong to the defendant";
- reports of examinations and tests that are material to the preparation of the defense; and
- written summaries of expert testimony that the government intends to use during its case-in-chief at trial.[20]

Rule 16 also imposes on the government a continuing duty to disclose additional evidence or material subject to discovery under the rule, if the government discovers such information prior to or during the trial.[21] Finally, Rule 16 grants the court discretion to issue sanctions or other orders "as are just" in the event the government fails to comply with a discovery request made under the rule.[22]

---

17. Napier Dewar, *supra* note 13 (proposing that when evidence that should have been disclosed earlier emerges during or shortly before trial, the court should consider instructing the jury on the duty to disclose and allowing the defendant to argue that failure to disclose raises a reasonable doubt about the defendant's guilt).
18. Fed. R. Crim. P. 16 Advisory Committee's Note (italics added).
19. *Id.*
20. Fed. R. Crim. P. 16(a)(1)(A)–(G).
21. Fed. R. Crim. P. 16(c).
22. Fed. R. Crim. P. 16(d)(2).

3. Federal Rule of Criminal Procedure 11

Federal Rule of Criminal Procedure 11 governs prosecutor and defendant practices during plea negotiations. The Supreme Court has not said whether disclosure of exculpatory evidence is required in the context of plea negotiations; however, in *United States v. Ruiz*, the Court held that the government is not constitutionally required to disclose *impeachment* evidence to a defendant prior to entering a plea agreement.[23] The Court noted that "impeachment information is special in relation to the *fairness of a trial,* not in respect to whether a plea is *voluntary* ('knowing,' 'intelligent,' and 'sufficiently aware')."[24] The Court stated that "[t]he degree of help that impeachment information can provide will depend upon the defendant's own independent knowledge of the prosecution's potential case—a matter that the Constitution does not require prosecutors to disclose."[25] Finally, the Court stated that "a constitutional obligation to provide impeachment information during plea bargaining, prior to entry of a guilty plea, could seriously interfere with the Government's interest in securing those guilty pleas that are factually justified, desired by defendants, and help to secure the efficient administration of justice."[26]

Since *Ruiz*, several courts have reviewed cases regarding impeachment evidence and *Brady* obligations.[27] Specifically, one court held that in circumstances where the government has failed to disclose impeachment evidence that is also exculpatory to the defense to prepare for trial in the hopes of executing a plea agreement, the withholding of *Brady* materials is "impermissible conduct by the government depriving [the defendant] of his ability to decide intelligently whether to plead guilty."[28]

---

23. 536 U.S. 622, 633 (2002).
24. *Id.* at 629 (quoting Brady v. United States, 397 U.S. 742, 748 (1970)).
25. *Id.* at 630.
26. *Id.* at 631.
27. *See* McCann v. Mangialardi, 337 F.3d 782, 788 (7th Cir. 2003) (stating it is likely to be violative of due process if prosecutors or relevant government actors are aware of the criminal defendant's factual innocence but fail to disclose such information to a defendant before he enters a guilty plea); United States v. Ohiri, 133 Fed. Appx. 555, 562 (10th Cir. 2005) (unpublished decision) (the court distinguished *Ruiz* holding that the government may not avoid the consequence of a *Brady* violation if the defendant accepts an eleventh-hour plea agreement without knowledge of withheld exculpatory evidence in the government's possession); Ferrara v. United States, 384 F. Supp. 2d 384, 414–15 (D. Mass. 2005) (asserting that where the intelligent character of a guilty plea is undermined by material misrepresentations or other prejudicial misconduct by the government, the plea may be vacated in a habeas corpus proceeding).
28. *Ferrara*, 384 F. Supp. 2d at 389.

4. American College of Trial Lawyers' proposal

In October 2003, the American College of Trial Lawyers (ACTL) proposed amending Federal Rules of Criminal Procedure 11 and 16 in order to "codify the rule of law first propounded in *Brady v. Maryland*, clarify both the nature and scope of favorable information, require the attorney for the government to exercise due diligence in locating information and establish deadlines by which the United States must disclose favorable information."[29]

5. Department of Justice's response to the ACTL's proposal

The Department of Justice (DOJ) opposed the ACTL's proposal to amend Federal Rules of Criminal Procedure 11 and 16. DOJ contended that the government's *Brady* obligations are "clearly defined by existing law that is the product of more than four decades of experience with the *Brady* rule," and therefore no codification of the *Brady* rule was warranted.[30]

6. Summary of Advisory Committee's and Department of Justice's work on amending Rule 16

In 2003, prompted by the American College of Trial Lawyers' proposal, the committee commenced discussions regarding whether an amendment was needed to Rule 16. Specifically, the committee explored whether Rule 16 should codify and expand the government's disclosure obligations regarding exculpatory and impeachment evidence favorable to the defense. Since that time, DOJ has continually opposed any proposed amendment to Rule 16, believing it to be unnecessary and expressing *inter alia* concern about pretrial disclosure of the identity of prosecution witnesses. Notwithstanding that position, DOJ has worked with the committee in drafting language for a proposed amendment while simultaneously undertaking efforts to revise the *U.S. Attorneys' Manual* (*Manual*) regarding the government's disclosure obligations that might serve as an alternative to an amendment to Rule 16.

On September 5, 2006, the committee met in special session by teleconference to discuss DOJ's proposed revision to the *Manual* and to decide whether, given the proposal, the committee should still forward the draft Rule 16 amendment to the Standing Committee for publication.

---

29. Memorandum from American College of Trial Lawyers to the Judicial Conference Advisory Committee on Federal Rules of Criminal Procedure (October 2003), at 2.

30. Memorandum from U.S. Department of Justice (Criminal Division) to Hon. Susan C. Bucklew, Chair, Judicial Conference Subcommittee on Rules 11 and 16 (April 26, 2004), at 2.

Committee minutes revealed that some committee members believed the revised language to the *Manual* was a substantial improvement, but in the end concluded that DOJ's internal policy could not serve as a substitute for the proposed amendment to Rule 16. Specifically, some members had concerns about the subjective language limiting the obligation to disclose impeachment materials to information the prosecutor sees as "significant" or "substantial." Additionally, one member commented that, even if the proposed provisions were identical, the fundamental question was whether the policy on disclosure of exculpatory and impeaching information should be solely an internal "Department" matter or should also be included in a rule. Further, there was concern that the policy was limited to prosecutors and did not alter or supersede the narrower *Giglio* policy applicable to investigators and other government agencies. Lastly, another member noted that the internal policy was not judicially enforceable and thus probably would not alter current practices. That member further added, "only the rule would provide an effective remedy for violation and actually reduce the number of problems in this area."

Several members favored an incremental approach and recommended that the committee defer consideration of a Rule 16 amendment until the impact of DOJ's proposed revision to the *Manual* could be assessed.

At the conclusion of the special session, the committee voted 8–4 to forward the proposed Rule 16 amendment to the Standing Committee for publication.[31] The proposed amendment creates a new subdivision and is based on the principle that fundamental fairness is enhanced when the defense has access before trial to any exculpatory and impeaching information known to the prosecution.

On October 19, 2006, DOJ posted a new *Manual* provision requiring greater disclosure of material and exculpatory evidence.[32]

B. Summary of Findings

- Thirty-seven of the ninety-four districts reported having a relevant local rule, order, or procedure specifically governing disclosure of *Brady* material. References to *Brady* material are usually in the courts' local rules but are also in courts' standard pretrial orders and scheduling orders. The remaining districts have not adopted any formal standards or rules that provide guidance to prosecutors on

---

31. *See* Appendix A.
32. *See* Appendix D. Contained within the *Manual* are general policies and procedures applicable to U.S. attorneys. The *Manual*'s primary function is to provide internal Department of Justice guidance.

discharging *Brady* obligations. These districts routinely follow Federal Rule of Criminal Procedure 16 or a local rule that mirrors Rule 16.
- Nineteen of the thirty-seven districts that explicitly reference *Brady* material use the term "favorable to the defendant" in describing evidence subject to the disclosure obligation. Nine districts refer to it by case name ("*Brady* material"). The remaining nine districts refer to *Brady* material as evidence that is "exculpatory" in nature.
- Twenty-eight of the thirty-seven districts mandate automatic disclosure; nine dictate that the government provide such material only upon request of the defense. One district requires parties to address *Brady* material in a requested pretrial conference, and two districts presume that the defendant has requested disclosure unless the presumption is overcome.
- The thirty-seven districts that reference *Brady* material vary significantly in their timetables for disclosure of the material. The most common time frame is "within fourteen days of the arraignment," followed by "within seven days of the arraignment," and "within ten days of the arraignment." Some districts have no specified time requirements for disclosure, using terms such as "as soon as reasonably possible" or "before the trial."
- In thirty-one of the thirty-seven districts with *Brady*-related provisions, the disclosure obligation is a continuing one, such that if additional evidence is discovered during the trial or after initial disclosure, the defendant must be notified and provided with the new evidence. The most common time frame for which this newly additional material must be turned over is "immediately" followed by "promptly."
- Of the thirty-seven districts with policies governing *Brady* material, thirteen have due diligence requirements for prosecutors. Two districts have a certificate of compliance requirement.
- None of the districts specifies specific sanctions for nondisclosure by prosecutors, leaving any sanction determination and remedy to the discretion of the court.
- Nine of the thirty-seven districts that reference *Brady* have declination procedures for disclosure of specific types of information. These procedures vary by districts, but most require a writing describing the specific matters in question and the reasons for declining to make the necessary disclosures required by the local rule or order.

II. U.S. District Court Rules and Policies Addressing *Brady* Material

This section describes federal district courts' local rules, orders, and procedures that codify the *Brady* rule, define *Brady* material, and set the timing and conditions for disclosure of *Brady* material. In addition, we discuss provisions containing due diligence obligations of the government and specific sanctions, if any, for the government's failure to comply with disclosure procedures.

This report does not address the degree to which the court's rules and other policies describe what actually occurs in the district. Nor does it address the government's compliance with *Brady*. Providing that type of information would necessitate a different type of research study.

A. Research Methods

Like the 2004 Center report, the information presented in this updated report is derived from a number of sources, including district courts' local rules, orders, and policies, and other relevant material. The majority of this information came from the courts' individual websites. We also searched the Westlaw and Lexis-Nexis federal court rules and orders databases for relevant information.

For twenty-eight districts, the review of the court's website and the database searches yielded specific local rules and orders that relate to the *Brady* decision or that set forth guidance to the government regarding disclosure of *Brady* material. For nine districts for which our searches did not yield a relevant local rule or order, we contacted the clerks of court to request their assistance in locating any local rules or materials relating to the application of the *Brady* decision. Through those efforts we identified thirty-seven districts that clearly refer to *Brady* material in their local rules, orders, or procedures. The remaining courts without a specific local rule either follow Federal Rule of Criminal Procedure 16 or a local rule that mirrors Rule 16.

During our research, we found instances in which individual judges have incorporated *Brady* obligations into their pretrial orders. A sample of those orders can be found in Appendix C.[33] They are not included in the analysis of this report since our objective was not to look at individual judge practices but rather court-wide policies and procedures.

---

33. *See, e.g.,* D.D.C. (Judge Walton's order); M.D. Fla. (Judge Bucklew's and Judge Corrigan's orders); N.D. Iowa (Judge Bennett's order); and D.P.R. (Judge Cerezo's order).

Three districts did not respond to our requests for information.[34]

The thirty-seven districts that have local rules, orders, and procedures specifically addressing *Brady* material served as the basis of our analysis. We reviewed and analyzed each of the thirty-seven districts' materials to determine

- the types of information defined as *Brady* material;
- whether the material is disclosed automatically or only upon request;
- the timing of disclosure;
- whether the parties had a continuing duty to disclose;
- whether the parties had a due diligence requirement; and
- whether there are specific provisions authorizing sanctions for failure to disclose *Brady* material.

We also noted whether the districts had declination procedures.

B. Governing Rules, Orders, and Procedures

We found references to *Brady* material in various documents, including local rules, orders (including standing orders and standard discovery, arraignment, scheduling, and pretrial orders), and supplementary materials such as joint statements of discovery and checklists (including disclosure agreement checklists).

Provisions for obligations to disclose *Brady* material are contained in the documents listed in Table 1. We were unable to find information on each of the variables discussed here for all districts. Consequently, we provide information only where available.

C. Definition of *Brady* Material

Most disclosure rules, orders, and procedures in the thirty-seven districts that address the *Brady* decision define *Brady* material in a number of ways: as "evidence favorable to the defendant" (19 districts),[35] by case

---

34. District of Guam, Eastern District of Missouri, and District of Oregon.
35. M.D. Ala. Standing Order on Criminal Discovery § (1)(B); S.D. Ala. R. 16.13 § (b)(1)(B); D. Conn. Cr. R. Appx. § (A)(11); N.D. Fla. R. 26.3(D)(1); S.D. Fla. R. 88.10(D); N.D. Ga. Standard Pretrial Order § IV(B); S.D. Ga. Cr. R. 16.1(f); W.D. La. Criminal Scheduling Order § II(c)(1); W.D. Mich. Standing Order Regarding Discovery in Criminal Cases § D; W.D. Mo. Scheduling and Trial Order § VI(A); N.D.N.Y. R. Cr. P. 14.1 § (b)(2); D. N. Mar. I. Cr. R. 17.1.1(c); W.D. Okla. Joint Statement of Discovery Conference § 5; W.D. Pa. Cr. R. 16.1(F); E.D. Tenn. Discovery and Scheduling Order ¶ 15; M.D. Tenn. R. 16.01(d); D. Vt. R. 16.1(a)(2); W.D. Wash. Cr. R. 16(a)(1)(K); S.D. W. Va. Arraignment Order & Discovery Requests III(1)(H).

name, e.g., "*Brady* material" (9 districts);[36] and as "exculpatory evidence" (9 districts).[37]

Table 1. District Court Documents that Reference *Brady* Material[38]

Document	Number of Districts	Districts
Local rules	17	S.D. Ala., N.D. Cal., D. Conn., N.D. Fla., S.D. Fla., S.D. Ga., D. Haw., D. Mass., D.N.H., N.D.N.Y., E.D. N.C., D. N. Mar. I., W.D. Pa., M.D. Tenn., W.D. Wash., N.D. W. Va., E.D. Wis.
Standard pretrial order	6	E.D. Ark., M.D. Ga., N.D. Ga., W.D. La., D.N.D., D. Vt.
Standing order	4	M.D. Ala., E.D. Mich., W.D. Mich., D.N.J.
Discovery and scheduling order	2	E.D. Tenn., D. Kan.
Scheduling order	2	W.D. Ky., W.D. Mo.
Arraignment order and standard discovery request	1	S.D. W. Va.
Criminal progression order	1	D. Neb.
Disclosure agreement checklist	1	W.D. Tex.
Joint discovery statement	1	W.D. Okla.
Procedural order	1	D. Idaho
Standard order	1	D.N.M.

---

36. E.D. Ark. Pretrial Order; M.D. Ga. Standard Pretrial Order ¶ 4; D. Haw. Crim. R. 16.1(a)(7); D. Idaho Procedural Order § I(5)(A); D. Kan. General Order of Discovery and Scheduling ¶ 10; W.D. Ky. Scheduling Order § 2(B)(2); D. Neb. Order for the Progression of a Criminal Case § 3; D.N.H. R. 16.1(c); D.N.M. Standard Discovery Order § 6.

37. N.D. Cal. Crim. R. 17.1-1 § (b)(3); D. Mass. R. 116.2; E.D. Mich. Standing Order for Discovery and Inspection and Fixing Motion Cut-Off Date in Criminal Cases § 1(b); D.N.J. Order for Discovery and Inspection § 1(f); E.D.N.C. Crim. R. 16.1(b)(6); D.N.D. Criminal Pretrial Order § II(d); W.D. Tex. Parties' Disclosure Agreement Checklist; N.D. W. Va. R. Cr. P. 16.05; E.D. Wis. Crim. R. 16.1(b).

38. A number of districts cover *Brady* obligations in more than one document. We chose the document with the most comprehensive information.

1. Evidence favorable to the defendant

The most common definition of "evidence favorable to the defendant," found in nineteen of the thirty-seven districts that use the term, defines *Brady* material as any material or information that may be favorable to the defendant on the issues of guilt or punishment and that is within the scope (or meaning) of *Brady*.[39] Five of the nineteen districts add the qualifier "without regard to materiality."[40]

2. Exculpatory evidence or exculpatory material

Nine districts refer to *Brady* material as exculpatory in nature.[41] Of these nine districts, Massachusetts has the most detailed and expansive rule dealing with *Brady* material and exculpatory evidence. It defines exculpatory evidence as follows:

- Information that would tend directly to negate the defendant's guilt concerning any count in the indictment or information.

- Information that would cast doubt on the admissibility of evidence that the government anticipates offering in its case-in-chief and that could be subject to a motion to suppress or exclude, which would, if allowed, be appealable under 18 U.S.C. § 3731.

- A statement whether any promise, reward, or inducement has been given to any witness whom the government anticipates calling in its case-in-chief, identifying by name each such witness and each promise, reward, or inducement, and a copy of any promise, reward, or inducement reduced to writing.

- A copy of any criminal record of any witness identified by name whom the government anticipates calling in its case-in-chief.

---

39. M.D. Ala. Standing Order on Criminal Discovery § (1)(B); S.D. Ala. R. 16.13 § (b)(1)(B); D. Conn. Cr. R. Appx. § (A)(11); N.D. Fla. R. 26.3(D)(1); S.D. Fla. R. 88.10(D); N.D. Ga. Standard Pretrial Order § IV(B); S.D. Ga. Cr. R. 16.1(f); W.D. La. Criminal Scheduling Order § II(c)(1); W.D. Mich. Standing Order Regarding Discovery in Criminal Cases § D; W.D. Mo. Scheduling and Trial Order § VI(A); N.D.N.Y. R. Cr. P. 14.1 § (b)(2); D. N. Mar. I. Cr. R. 17.1.1(c); W.D. Okla. Joint Statement of Discovery Conference § 5; W.D. Pa. Cr. R. 16.1(F); E.D. Tenn. Discovery and Scheduling Order ¶ 15; M.D. Tenn. R. 16.01(d); D. Vt. R. 16.1(a)(2); W.D. Wash. Cr. R. 16(a)(1)(K); S.D. W. Va. Arraignment Order & Discovery Requests III(1)(H).

40. M.D. Ala. Standing Order on Criminal Discovery § (1)(B); S.D. Ala. R. 16.13 § (b)(1)(B); D. Conn. Cr. R. Appx. § (A)(11); N.D. Fla. R. 26.3(D)(1); D. Vt. R. 16.1(a)(2).

41. N.D. Cal. Crim. R. 17.1-1 § (b)(3); D. Mass. R. 116.2; E.D. Mich. Standing Order for Discovery and Inspection and Fixing Motion Cut-Off Date in Criminal Cases § 1(b); D.N.J. Order for Discovery and Inspection § 1(f); E.D.N.C. Crim. R. 16.1(b)(6); D.N.D. Criminal Pretrial Order § II(d); W.D. Tex. Parties' Disclosure Agreement Checklist; N.D. W. Va. R. Crim. P. 16.05; E.D. Wis. Crim. R. 16.1(b) & (c).

- A written description of any criminal cases pending against any witness identified by name whom the government anticipates calling in its case-in-chief.
- A written description of the failure of any percipient witness identified by name to make a positive identification of a defendant, if any identification procedure has been held with such a witness with respect to the crime at issue.
- Any information that tends to cast doubt on the credibility or accuracy of any witness whom or evidence that the government anticipates calling or offering in its case-in-chief.
- Any inconsistent statement, or a description of such a statement, made orally or in writing by any witness whom the government anticipates calling in its case-in-chief, regarding the alleged criminal conduct of the defendant.
- Any statement, or a description of such a statement, made orally or in writing by any person, that is inconsistent with any statement made orally or in writing by any witness the government anticipates calling in its case-in-chief, regarding the alleged criminal conduct of the defendant.
- Information reflecting bias or prejudice against the defendant by any witness whom the government anticipates calling in its case-in-chief.
- A written description of any prosecutable federal offense known by the government to have been committed by any witness whom the government anticipates calling in its case-in-chief.
- A written description of any conduct that may be admissible under Fed. R. Evid. 608(b) known by the government to have been committed by a witness whom the government anticipates calling in its case-in-chief.
- Information known to the government of any mental or physical impairment of any witness whom the government anticipates calling in its case-in-chief, that may cast doubt on the ability of that witness to testify accurately or truthfully at trial as to any relevant event.
- Exculpatory information regarding any witness or evidence that the government intends to offer in rebuttal.
- A written summary of any information in the government's possession that tends to diminish the degree of the defendant's culpability or the defendant's Offense Level under the United States Sentencing Guidelines.[42]

---

42. D. Mass. R. 116.2(B).

3. Brady material generally

Nine districts cite only to *Brady v. Maryland* or to *Brady* and some other case authority when addressing the prosecutor's obligation to turn over exculpatory material.[43]

D. Disclosure Requirements

Twenty-eight districts mandate automatic disclosure of *Brady* material.[44] One district, the Middle District of Georgia, has a caveat—the government need not furnish the defendant with *Brady* information that the defendant has obtained or, with reasonable diligence, could obtain himself or herself.[45] Another district, the Western District of Kentucky, requires that "[i]f the United States has knowledge of *Brady* rule evidence and is unsure as to the nature of the evidence and the proper time for disclosure, it may request an *in camera* hearing for the purpose of resolving this issue."[46]

Nine districts dictate that the government provide *Brady* material upon request of the defendant.[47] The Northern District of California adds qualifying language that requires that the parties address the issue "if pertinent

---

43. E.D. Ark. Pretrial Order; M.D. Ga. Standard Pretrial Order ¶ 4; D. Haw. Crim. R. 16.1(a)(7); D. Idaho Procedural Order § I(5)(A); D. Kan. General Order of Discovery and Scheduling ¶ 10; W.D. Ky. Scheduling Order § 2(B)(2); D. Neb. Order for the Progression of a Criminal Case § 3; D.N.H. R. 16.1(c); D.N.M. Standard Discovery Order § 6.

44. M.D. Ala. Standing Order on Criminal Discovery § (1)(B); S.D. Ala. R. 16.13 § (b)(1)(B); E.D. Ark. Pretrial Order; D. Conn. Cr. R. Appx. § (A)(11); N.D. Fla. R. 26.3(D)(1); S.D. Fla. R. 88.10(D); D. Haw. Crim. R. 16.1(a)(7); D. Kan. General Order of Discovery and Scheduling ¶ 10; W.D. Ky. Scheduling Order § 2(B)(2); D. Mass. R. 116.2; E.D. Mich. Standing Order for Discovery and Inspection and Fixing Motion Cut-Off Date in Criminal Cases § 1(b); W.D. Mich. Standing Order Regarding Discovery in Criminal Cases § D; W.D. Mo. Scheduling and Trial Order § VI(A); D. Neb. Order for the Progression of a Criminal Case § 3; D.N.H. R. 16.1(c); D.N.J. Order for Discovery and Inspection § 1(f); D.N.M. Standard Discovery Order § 6; N.D.N.Y. R. Cr. P. 14.1 § (b)(2); D.N.D. Criminal Pretrial Order § II(d); D. N. Mar. I. Cr. R. 17.1.1(c); W.D. Okla. Joint Statement of Discovery Conference § 5; W.D. Pa. Cr. R. 16.1(F); E.D. Tenn. Discovery and Scheduling Order ¶ 15; M.D. Tenn. R. 16.01(d); W.D. Tex. Parties' Disclosure Agreement Checklist; D. Vt. R. 16.1(a)(2); N.D. W. Va. R. Cr. P. 16.05; E.D. Wis. Crim. R. 16.1(b).

45. M.D. Ga. Standard Pretrial Order ¶ 5 (citing United States v. Slocum, 708 F.2d 587, 599 (11th Cir. 1983)).

46. W.D. Ky. Scheduling Order § 4.

47. N.D. Cal. Crim. R. 17.1-1 § (b)(3); M.D. Ga. Standard Pretrial Order ¶ 5; N.D. Ga. Standard Magistrate Judge's Pretrial Order § IV(B); S.D. Ga. Crim. R. 16.1(f); D. Idaho Procedural Order § I(5); W.D. La. Criminal Scheduling Order § II(c); E.D.N.C. Crim. R. 16.1(b)(6); W.D. Wash. Crim. R. 16(a)(1)(K); S.D. W. Va. Arraignment Order and Standard Discovery Request § III(1)(H).

to the case" and in their pretrial conference statement "if a conference is held."[48]

Only one district, the Middle District of Tennessee, specifically addresses the disposition of the information or evidence once the case has been resolved. That district requires that the information or evidence be returned to the "government or destroyed following the completion of the trial, sentencing of the defendant, or completion of the direct appellate process, whichever occurs last."[49] A party who destroys materials must certify the destruction by letter to the government.

1. *Time requirements for disclosure*[50]

The thirty-seven districts vary significantly in their disclosure timetables. Some districts specify a time by which the prosecution must disclose *Brady* material, while other districts rely on nonspecific terms such as "in time for effective use at trial" or "as soon as reasonably possible."

a. Specific time requirement

Thirty-three districts have mandated time limits (or specific events, such as arraignments or pretrial conferences) for prosecutorial disclosure of *Brady* material (see Table 2).

---

48. N.D. Cal. Crim. R. 17.1-1(b).
49. M.D. Tenn. Crim. R. 16.02.
50. It is well settled that the district court may order when *Brady* material is to be disclosed. *See* United States v. Starusko, 729 F.2d 256 (3d Cir. 1984). Some decisions have held that the Jencks Act controls and that *Brady* material relating to a certain witness need not be disclosed until that witness has testified on direct examination at trial. United States v. Bencs, 28 F.3d 555 (6th Cir. 1994); United States v. Jones, 612 F.2d 453 (9th Cir. 1979); United States v. Scott, 524 F.2d 465 (5th Cir. 1975). Others have held that *Brady* material might be disclosed prior to trial, in order to afford the defendant the opportunity to make effective use of the material during trial. *See* United States v. Perez, 870 F.2d 1222 (7th Cir. 1989); United States v. Campagnuolo, 592 F.2d 852 (5th Cir. 1979); United States v. Pollack, 534 F.2d 964 (D.C. Cir. 1976).

Table 2. Districts with Time Requirements for Prosecutorial Disclosure of *Brady* Material

Time Requirement	Number of Districts	Districts
Within 14 days of arraignment	5	N.D.N.Y,[51] S.D. Fla.,[52] M.D. Tenn., W.D. Tex.,[53] D. Vt.[54]
Within 7 days of arraignment	4	D. Hawaii,[55] D. Idaho, W.D. Mich., N.D. W. Va.
Within 10 days of arraignment	4	D. Conn., E.D. Mich.,[56] W.D. Mo., D. Neb.[57]
At arraignment	3	M.D. Ala., S.D. Ala., E.D. Wis.
Within 5 days of arraignment	3	N.D. Fla., S.D. Ga., W.D. Pa.
At pretrial conference	2	E.D.N.C.,[58] D. N. Mar. I.[59]
Within a reasonable time after arraignment	1	D. Kan.
Within 28 days of arraignment	1	D. Mass.
At discovery conference	1	W.D. Wash.
10 days after not guilty plea	1	W.D. Okla.
10–20 days after not guilty plea	1	N.D. Cal.
10 days after defendant's request	1	S.D. W. Va.
7 days after court's order	1	W.D. Ky.[60]
8 days after court's order	1	D.N.M.
10 days after court's order	1	D.N.J.

---

51. Or on the date the court otherwise sets for good cause.
52. Or as ordered by the court.
53. If defendant waives the arraignment within fourteen days after latest arraignment date.
54. Or date otherwise set by court.
55. Government must file and serve notice of compliance with discovery.
56. Or other date set by judge.
57. Upon request for additional discovery or disputed *Brady* materials "as soon as practicable upon request."
58. May exchange by mail. "Rule adds to government disclosure obligations under Rule 16, and requires the scheduling of a pretrial conference at which Rule 16 materials should be given to a defendant." United States v. King, 121 F.R.D. 277 (E.D.N.C. 1988).
59. Conference upon request or *sua sponte*.
60. If not prior to order then *Brady* disclosure must be in time for effective use at trial.

Time Requirement	Number of Districts	Districts
14 days after court's order	1	E.D. Tenn.[61]
20 days before trial	1	D.N.H.[62]
Not less than 7 days before trial	1	W.D. La.[63]

b. No specific time requirement

Four districts have nonspecific time requirements for disclosure, set out in local rules or in various court orders. The terms used for these time requirements include the following descriptions:

- "in time for effective use at trial";[64]
- "as soon as reasonably possible";[65]
- "sufficiently in advance of trial to allow a defendant to use it effectively";[66] and
- "discovery shall be accomplished without the necessity of court intervention."[67]

2. *Duration of disclosure requirements*

Thirty-one of the thirty-seven districts make the prosecutor's disclosure obligation a continuing one, such that if additional evidence is discovered during the trial or after initial disclosure, the defendant must be notified and shown the new evidence.[68] Many of the districts use adjectives or

---

61. In the Eastern District of Tennessee, timing of disclosure is governed by *United States v. Presser*, 844 F.2d 1275 (6th Cir. 1988), which addressed material that was arguably exempt from pretrial disclosure by the Jencks Act, yet also arguably exculpatory under the *Brady* rule. There, the material needed only to be disclosed to defendants "in time for use at trial."

62. For good cause shown the government may seek approval to disclose said material at a later time.

63. Parties must meet in person.

64. E.D. Ark. Pretrial Order for Criminal Cases.

65. M.D. Ga. Standard Pretrial Order ¶ 5.

66. N.D. Ga. Standard Criminal Pretrial Order IV.B.

67. D.N.D. Criminal Pretrial Order § II(a).

68. M.D. Ala. Standing Order on Criminal Discovery § Supplementation; S.D. Ala. R. 16.13 § (c); E.D. Ark. Pretrial Order; D. Conn. Cr. R. Appx. § (D); N.D. Fla. R. 26.3(G)(2); S.D. Fla. R. 88.10(Q)(3); N.D. Ga. Standard Pretrial Order § IV(A); S.D. Ga. Cr. R. 16.1(g); D. Haw. Crim. R. 16.1(c); D. Idaho Procedural Order § I(5); D. Kan. General Order of Discovery and Scheduling; W.D. Ky. Scheduling Order § 2(B)(2); W.D. La. Criminal Scheduling Order § II(c)(8); D. Mass. R. 116.7; E.D. Mich. Standing Order for Discovery and Inspection and Fixing Motion Cut-Off Date in Criminal Cases § (3); W.D. Mich. Standing Order Regarding Discovery in Criminal Cases § M; M.D. Neb. Order for the Progression of a Criminal Case § 2; D.N.H. R. 16.2; D.N.J. Order for Dis-

modifiers to more clearly define how soon after discovery of new material the government must disclose it.[69] Nine of the thirty-one districts provide no timing information.[70]

E. Due Diligence Requirements

Thirteen districts have "due diligence" requirements for prosecutors regarding discovery.[71] One district[72] requires the government to sign and file a "certificate of compliance" (with *Brady* obligations) with discovery. Another district obliges the parties to "collaborate in preparation of a written statement to be signed by counsel for each side, generally describing all discovery material exchanged, and setting forth all stipulations entered into at the conference."[73]

While other districts do not use the term "due diligence" in their local rules, orders, or procedures, some make it clear that the government has the responsibility to identify and produce discoverable evidence and information. For example, the Western District of Missouri's rule regarding

---

covery and Inspection § 5; D.N.M. Standard Discovery Order § 4; N.D.N.Y. R. Cr. P. 14.1 § (f); E.D.N.C. Crim. R. 16.1(e); D.N.D. Criminal Pretrial Order § II; W.D. Okla. Joint Statement of Discovery Conference § 5; E.D. Tenn. Discovery and Scheduling Order ¶ 16; M.D. Tenn. R. 16.01(n); W.D. Tex. R. CR-16(b)(4); D. Vt. R. 16.1(e); W.D. Wash. Cr. R. 16(a)(2)(E)(d); N.D. W. Va. R. Cr. P. 16.12; S.D. W. Va. R. Cr. P. 16.1(f).

69. *E.g.*, "immediately" (D. Conn. Crim. R. App. Standing Order on Discovery § D; S.D. Fla. Gen. R. 88.10; D. Kan. General Order of Discovery and Scheduling; W.D. La. Criminal Scheduling Order § II(c)(8); W.D. Mich. Standing Order Regarding Discovery in Criminal Cases § M; E.D. Tenn. Discovery and Scheduling Order ¶ 16; M.D. Tenn. R. 16.01(n); N.D. W. Va. R. Crim. P. 16.05); "promptly" (E.D. Ark. Pretrial Order; D. Haw. Crim. R. 16.1(c); D. Mass. R. 116.7; D.N.M. Standard Discovery Order § 4; W.D. Tex. R. CR-16(b)(4); D. Vt. R. 16.1(e); W.D. Wash. Cr. R. 16(a)(2)(E)(d)); "expeditiously" (M.D. Ala. Standing Order on Criminal Discovery; S.D. Ala. R. 16.13(c); N.D.N.Y. R. Crim. P. 14.1(f); "as soon as it is received" (S.D. W. Va. R. Cr. P. 16.1(f)); "as soon as practicable" (D. Idaho Procedural Order § I(5)); "by the speediest means available" (N.D. Fla. Crim. R. 26.3(G)); and "when information is discovered" (D.N.H. R. 16.2).

70. E.D. Ark. Pretrial Order; N.D. Ga. Standard Pretrial Order § IV(A); S.D. Ga. Cr. R. 16.1; W.D. Ky. Arraignment Order Reciprocal Order of Discovery (Louisville Division) 3(c); E.D. Mich. Standing Order for Discovery and Inspection and Fixing Motion Cut-Off Date in Criminal Cases § 3(f); D. Neb. Order for the Progression of a Criminal Case; D.N.J. Order for Discovery and Inspection § 3; E.D.N.C. Crim. R. 16.1(e); W.D. Okla. Joint Statement of Discovery Conference.

71. D. Conn. Crim. R. App. Standing Order on Discovery § A; S.D. Fla. R. 88.10(A); D. Haw. Crim. R. 16.1; D. Mass. R. 116.2(A)(1); W.D. Mich. Standing Order Regarding Discovery in Criminal Cases §§ A & B; W.D. Mo. Scheduling and Trial Order § I; D.N.H. Crim. R. 16.2; D.N.M. Standard Discovery Order § 2; E.D.N.C. Crim. R. 16.1(b)(1); E.D. Tenn. Discovery and Scheduling Order § A; M.D. Tenn. R. 16.01(a)(2); W.D. Wash. Crim. R. 16(a); N.D. W. Va. R. Cr. P. 16.01(a).

72. W.D. Mo. Scheduling and Trial Order § IX.

73. W.D. Mich. Standing Order Regarding Discovery in Criminal Cases § L.

the government's responsibility for reviewing the case file for *Brady* (and *Giglio*) material provides:

> The government is advised that if any portion of the government's investigative file or that of any investigating agency is not made available to the defense for inspection, the Court will expect that trial counsel for the government or an attorney under trial counsel's immediate supervision who is familiar with the *Brady/Giglio* doctrine will have reviewed the applicable files for the purpose of ascertaining whether evidence favorable to the defense is contained in the file.[74]

In addition, the Middle and Southern Districts of Alabama include a restriction on the delegation of the responsibility:

> The identification and production of all discoverable information and evidence is the personal responsibility of the Assistant U.S. Attorney assigned to the action and may not be delegated without the express permission of the Court.[75]

F. Sanctions for Noncompliance with *Brady* Obligations

None of the thirty-seven districts specifies remedies for prosecutorial nondisclosure. All leave the determination of any sanctions to the discretion of the court.

However, several districts provide some guidance for judges dealing with the failure of the government to comply with *Brady/Giglio* obligations. The Uniform Procedural Order in the District of Idaho provides:

> If the government has information in its possession at the time of the arraignment, but elects not to disclose this information until a later time in the proceedings, the court can consider this as one factor in determining whether the defendant can make effective use of the information at trial.[76]

The Eastern District of Michigan's rule notes "the government proceeds at its peril if there is a failure to disclose information pursuant to Rule 16(a)(1) and exculpatory evidence."[77] And the Western District of Kentucky's rule states that the "[f]ailure to disclose *Brady* [material] at a time when it can be used effectively may result in a recess or continuance so that defendant may properly utilize such evidence."[78]

---

74. W.D. Mo. Scheduling and Trial Order Note following §§ VI(A) & (B).
75. M.D. Ala. Standing Order on Criminal Discovery § 2(C); S.D. Ala. R. 16.13(b)(2)(C).
76. D. Idaho Procedural Order § I(5).
77. E.D. Mich. Standing Order for Discovery and Inspection and Fixing Motion Cut-Off Date in Criminal Cases § 1(b).
78. W.D. Ky. Scheduling Order § 2(B)(2).

Most courts allow sanctions (generally based on Rule 16's authority) for both parties for general discovery abuses. These sanctions include exclusion of evidence at trial, a finding of contempt, granting a continuance, and even dismissal of the indictment with prejudice. For example, the Northern District of West Virginia's local rule provides:

> If at any time during the course of the proceedings it is brought to the attention of the Court that a party has failed to comply with L.R. Crim. P. 16 [the general discovery rule], the Court may order such party to permit the discovery or inspection, grant a continuance or prohibit the party from introducing evidence not disclosed, or the Court may enter such order as it deems just under the circumstances up to and including the dismissal of the indictment with prejudice.[79]

G. Declination Procedures

Nine of the thirty-seven districts specifically refer to declination procedures in their local rules or orders.[80] Procedures vary by districts, but most require a writing describing the specific matters in question and the reasons for declining to make the necessary disclosures required by the local rule or order. For example, the Southern District of Georgia's local rule says:

> In the event the U.S. Attorney declines to furnish any such information described in this rule, he shall file such declination in writing specifying the types of disclosure that are declined and the ground therefor. If defendant's attorney objects to such refusal, he shall move the Court for a hearing therein.[81]

The District of Massachusetts has an even more detailed rule governing the declination of disclosure and protective orders, providing for challenges, sealed filings, and ex parte motions:

> (A) Declination. If in the judgment of a party it would be detrimental to the interests of justice to make any of the disclosures required by these Local Rules, such disclosures may be declined, before or at the time that disclosure is due, and the opposing party advised in writing, with a copy filed in the Clerk's Office, of the specific matters on which disclosure is declined and the reasons for declining. If the op-

---

79. N.D. W. Va. R. Crim. P. 16.11.
80. S.D. Ga. Crim. R. 16.1(g); W.D. Ky. Arraignment Order Reciprocal Order of Discovery (Louisville Division) 3(c); W.D. La. Criminal Scheduling Order § III(a); D. Mass. R. 116.6(A); E.D. Mich. Standing Order for Discovery and Inspection and Fixing Motion Cut-Off Date in Criminal Cases § (2); D.N.J. Order for Discovery and Inspection § 2; W.D. Pa. Cr. R. 16.1(B); W.D. Wash. Crim. R. 16(e); N.D. W. Va. R. Cr. P. 16.02.
81. S.D. Ga. Crim. R. 16.1(g).

posing party seeks to challenge the declination, that party shall file a motion to compel that states the reasons why disclosure is sought. Upon the filing of such motion, except to the extent otherwise provided by law, the burden shall be on the party declining disclosure to demonstrate, by affidavit and supporting memorandum citing legal authority, why such disclosure should not be made. The declining party may file its submissions in support of declination under seal pursuant to L.R. 7.2 for the Court's in camera consideration. Unless otherwise ordered by the Court, a redacted version of each such submission shall be served on the moving party, which may reply.

(B) Ex Parte Motions for Protective Orders. This Local Rule does not preclude any party from moving under L.R. 7.2 and ex parte (i.e., without serving the opposing party) for leave to file an ex parte motion for a protective order with respect to any discovery matter. Nor does this Local Rule limit the Court's power to accept or reject an ex parte motion or to decide such a motion in any manner it deems appropriate.[82]

Four of the thirty-seven districts have procedures for motions to deny, modify, restrict, or defer discovery or inspection.[83] The moving party has the burden to show cause why discovery should be limited.

---

82. D. Mass. Crim. R. 116.6.
83. *See, e.g.,* D. Conn. Cr. R. Appx. § (F); W.D. Mich. Standing Order Regarding Discovery in Criminal Cases § N; E.D. Tenn. Discovery and Scheduling Order ¶ 17; M.D. Tenn. R. 16.01(n). The Middle District of Tennessee's local rule language is similar to Connecticut's; however, the Middle District of Tennessee's local rule includes the following cautionary message: "It is expected by the Court, however, that counsel for both sides shall make every good faith effort to comply with the letter and spirit of this Rule." M.D. Tenn. R. 16.01(a)(2)(n).

Appendix A
Proposed Rule 16 Amendment and Committee Note

March 15, 2006, draft

Rule 16. Discovery and Inspection
(a) GOVERNMENT'S DISCLOSURE.
  (1) *INFORMATION SUBJECT TO DISCLOSURE.*

* * * *

(H) *Exculpatory or Impeaching Information*. Upon a defendant's request, the government must make available all information that is known to the attorney for the government or agents of law enforcement involved in the investigation of the case that is either exculpatory or impeaching. The court may not order disclosure of impeachment information earlier than 14 days before trial.

COMMITTEE NOTE

Subdivision (a)(1)(H). New subdivision (a)(1)(H) is based on the principle that fundamental fairness is enhanced when the defense has access before trial to any exculpatory or impeaching information known to the prosecution. The requirement that exculpatory and impeaching information be provided to the defense also reduces the possibility that innocent persons will be convicted in federal proceedings. *See generally* ABA STANDARDS FOR CRIMINAL JUSTICE, PROSECUTION FUNCTION AND DEFENSE FUNCTION 3-3.11(a) (3d ed. 1993), and ABA MODEL RULE OF PROFESSIONAL CONDUCT 3.8(d) (2003). The amendment is intended to supplement the prosecutor's obligations to disclose material exculpatory or impeaching information under *Brady v. Maryland*, 373 U.S. 83 (1963), *Giglio v. United States*, 405 U.S. 150 (1972), *Kyles v. Whitley*, 514 U.S. 419 (1995), *Strickler v. Greene*, 527 U.S. 263, 280–81 (1999), and *Banks v. Dretke*, 540 U.S. 668, 691 (2004).

The rule contains no requirement that the information be "material" to guilt in the sense that this term is used in cases such as *Kyles v. Whitley*. It requires prosecutors to disclose to the defense all exculpatory or impeaching information known to any law enforcement agency that participated in the prosecution or investigation of the case without further speculation as to whether this information will ultimately be material to guilt.

The amendment distinguishes between exculpatory and impeaching information for purposes of the timing of disclosure. Information is exculpatory under the rule if it tends to cast doubt upon the defendant's guilt as to any essential element in any count in the indictment or information.

Because the disclosure of the identity of witnesses raises special concerns, and impeachment information may disclose a witness's identity, the rule provides that the court may not order the disclosure of information that is impeaching but not exculpatory earlier than 14 days before trial. The government may apply to the court for a protective order concerning exculpatory or impeaching information under the already-existing provision of Rule 16(d)(1), so as to defer disclosure to a later time.

Appendix B

Compendium of U.S. District Court Material Addressing *Brady* Material

Middle District of Alabama

STANDARD ORDER ON CRIMINAL DISCOVERY

... (1) Disclosure by the Government. At arraignment, or on a date otherwise set by the court for good cause shown, the government shall tender to defendant the following:

... (B) *Brady* Material. All information and material known to the government which may be favorable to the defendant on the issues of guilt or punishment, without regard to materiality, within the scope of *Brady v. Maryland*, 373 U.S. 83 (1963).

Southern District of Alabama

LR16.13 CRIMINAL DISCOVERY

... (b) Initial Disclosures.

... (B) *Brady* Material. All information and material known to the government which may be favorable to the defendant on the issues of guilt or punishment, without regard to materiality, within the scope of *Brady v. Maryland*, 373 U.S. 83 (1963).

Eastern District of Arkansas

PRETRIAL ORDER FOR CRIMINAL CASES

Brady/Giglio
The government must comply with its Constitutional obligation to disclose any information known to it that is material to the guilt or punishment of the defendant whether or not the defendant requests it. *Brady* and *Giglio* information must be disclosed in time for effective use at trial.

Northern District of California

17.1-1. PRETRIAL CONFERENCE

... (b) Pretrial Conference Statement. Unless otherwise ordered, not less than 4 days prior to the pretrial conference, the parties shall file a pretrial conference statement addressing the matters set forth below, if pertinent to the case:

... (3) Disclosure of exculpatory or other evidence favorable to the defendant on the issue of guilt or punishment ...

District of Connecticut

APPENDIX STANDING ORDER ON DISCOVERY

In all criminal cases, it is Ordered:

(A) Disclosure by the Government. Within ten (10) days from the date of arraignment, government and defense counsel shall meet, at which time the attorney for the government shall furnish copies, or allow defense counsel to inspect or listen to and record items which are impractical to copy, of the following items in the possession, custody or control of the government, the existence of which is known or by the exercise of due diligence may become known to the attorney for the government or to the agents responsible for the investigation of the case:

... (11) All information known to the government which may be favorable to the defendant on the issues of guilt or punishment within the scope of *Brady v. Maryland*, 373 U.S. 83 (1963).

Northern District of Florida

Rule 26.3. DISCOVERY – CRIMINAL

... (D) *Other Disclosure Obligations of the Government.*—The government's attorney shall provide the following within five (5) days after the defendant's arraignment, or promptly after acquiring knowledge thereof:

(1) *Brady* Material.—All information and material known to the government which may be favorable to the defendant on the issues of guilt or punishment, without regard to materiality, that is within the scope of *Brady v. Maryland, 373 U.S. 83 (1963)* and *United States v. Agurs, 427 U.S. 97 (1976).*

Southern District of Florida

Rule 88.10. CRIMINAL DISCOVERY

... C. The government shall reveal to the defendant and permit inspection and copying of all information and material known to the government which may be favorable to the defendant on the issues of guilt or punishment within the scope of *Brady v. Maryland, 373 U.S. 83 (1963),* and *United States v. Agurs, 427 U.S. 97 (1976).*

Middle District of Georgia

DISCOVERY AND INSPECTION UNDER *BRADY* AND RULE 16; DISCLOSING IMPEACHING INFORMATION AND EXCULPATORY EVIDENCE

A defendant has a right only to discovery of evidence pursuant to Rule 16 of the Federal Rules of Criminal Procedure or *Brady v. Maryland*, 373 U.S. 83 (1963), and its progeny.

Northern District of Georgia

STANDARD CRIMINAL ORDER

. . . B. *Discovery and Disclosure of Evidence Arguably Subject to Suppression and of Evidence Which Is Exculpatory and/or Impeaching:* Upon request of the defendant, the government is directed to comply with FED. R. CRIM. P. 16 and with FED. R. CRIM. P. 12 by providing notice as specified in section II.B, *supra*. The government is also directed to provide all materials and information that are arguably favorable to the defendant in compliance with its obligations under *Brady v. Maryland*, 373 U.S. 83 (1963), *Giglio v. United States*, 405 U.S. 150 (1972), and their progeny. Exculpatory material as defined in *Brady* and *Kyles v. Whitley*, 514 U.S. 419, 434 (1995), must be provided sufficiently in advance of trial to allow a defendant to use it effectively. Impeachment material must be provided no later than production of the *Jencks* Act statements.

Southern District of Georgia

LCrR 16.1. PRETRIAL DISCOVERY AND INSPECTION IN CRIMINAL CASES

Within five (5) days after arraignment, the United States Attorney and the defendant's attorney shall confer and, upon request, the government shall:

. . . (f) Permit defendant's attorney to inspect and copy or photograph any evidence favorable to the defendant.

District of Hawaii

CrimLR 16.1. STANDING ORDER FOR ROUTINE DISCOVERY IN CRIMINAL CASES

... A request for discovery set out in this paragraph and in *Fed.R.Crim.P. 16* is entered for the defendant to the government by this rule so that the defendant need not make a further request for such discovery. If the defendant does not request such discovery, he or she shall file a notice to the government that he or she does not request such discovery within five (5) days after arraignment. If such a notice is filed, the government is relieved of any discovery obligations to the defendant imposed by this paragraph or *Fed.R.Crim.P. 16*. If the defendant does not file such a notice, within seven (7) days after arraignment unless otherwise ordered by the court or promptly upon subsequent discovery, the government shall permit the defendant to inspect and copy or photograph, or, in the case of the defendant's criminal record, shall furnish a copy, and provide the information listed in the subparagraphs enumerated immediately below. Upon providing the information required in the enumerated subparagraphs below, the government shall file and serve notice of compliance with discovery mandated under this paragraph.

... 7. *Brady* material, as it shall be presumed that defendant has made a general *Brady v. Maryland, 373 U.S. 83, 83 S. Ct. 1194, 10 L. Ed. 2d 215, 1963 U.S. LEXIS 1615 (1963)* request. Specific requests shall be made in writing to the government or by motion ...

District of Idaho

PROCEDURAL ORDER

... 5. The Court strongly encourages the government to produce any information currently in its possession and described in the following paragraphs within seven (7) calendar days of the date of the arraignment on the indictment, in conjunction with the material being produced under Part I, paragraph 1 of this Procedural Order. As to any materials not currently in the possession of the government, including information that may not be exculpatory in nature at the time of the arraignment but as the case proceeds towards trial may become exculpatory because of subsequent events, then the government shall, as soon as practicable and at a minimum for the defendant to make effective use of it at trial, disclose the information. If the government has information in its possession at the time of the arraignment, but elects not to disclose this information until a later time in the proceedings, the court can consider this as one factor in determining whether the defendant can make effective use of the information at trial.

A. Disclose all material evidence within the scope of *Brady v. Maryland*, 373 U.S. 83 (1963), *United States v. Agurs*, 427 U.S. 97 (1976), and *Kyles v. Whitley*, 514 U.S. 419 (1995), and their progeny.

District of Kansas

GENERAL ORDER OF SCHEDULING AND DISCOVERY

. . . In general, the court will order the parties to comply with Rules 12, 12.1, 12.2, 16 and 26.2 of the Federal Rules of Criminal Procedure, with *Brady v. Maryland*, 373 U.S. 83, 83 S. Ct. 1194 (1963), *Giglio v. United States*, 405 U.S. 150, 92 S. Ct. 763 (1972) and their progeny, and with Title 18, U.S.C. § 3500, as well as Rule 404(b), Federal Rules of Evidence. A request is not necessary to trigger the operation of the Rules and the absence of a request may not be asserted as a reason for noncompliance.

. . . Within a reasonable time period after arraignment, the government shall comply with Rules 12(b)(4)(B) and 16, and *Brady/Giglio*. Pursuant to Rule 16, the government shall copy for the defendant or permit the defendant to inspect and copy or photograph:

. . . Pursuant to *Brady* and *Giglio* and their progeny, the government shall produce any and all evidence in its possession, custody or control which would tend to exculpate the defendant (that is, evidence which is favorable and material to a defense), or which would constitute impeachment of government witnesses, or which would serve to mitigate punishment, if any, which may be imposed in this case. This includes and is not limited to the following:

1. Any evidence tending to show threats, promises, payments or inducements made by the government or any agent thereof which would bear upon the credibility of any government witness.

2. Any statement of any government witness which is inconsistent with a statement by the witness which led to the indictment in this case.

3. Any statement of any government witness which the attorney for the government knows or reasonably believes will be inconsistent with the witness' testimony at trial.

4. Any prior conviction of any government witness, which involved dishonesty or false statement, or for which the penalty was death or imprisonment in excess of one year under the law under which he was convicted.

5. Any pending felony charges against any government witness.

6. Any specific instances of the conduct of any government witness which would tend to show character for untruthfulness.

Western District of Kentucky

SCHEDULING ORDER

. . . (2) *Brady material*. The government shall disclose any *Brady* material of which it has knowledge in the following manner:

(a) pretrial disclosure of any *Brady* material discoverable under Rule 16(a)(1);

(b) disclosure of all other *Brady* material in time for effective use at trial.

Western District of Louisiana
CRIMINAL SCHEDULING ORDER

. . . (c) Not less than 7 days prior to trial:

(1) The government shall reveal to the defendant and permit inspection and copying of all information and material known to the government which may be favorable to the defendant on the issues of guilt or punishment within the scope of *Brady v. Maryland*, *United States v. Agurs*, and *Kyles v. Whitley*.

District of Massachusetts
RULE 116.1 DISCOVERY IN CRIMINAL CASES

(A) Discovery Alternatives.

(1) Automatic Discovery. In all felony cases, unless a defendant waives automatic discovery, all discoverable material and information in the possession, custody, or control of the government and that defendant, the existence of which is known, or by the exercise of due diligence may become known, to the attorneys for those parties, must be disclosed to the opposing party without formal motion practice at the times and under the automatic discovery procedures specified in this Local Rule.

. . . (C) Automatic Discovery Provided By The Government.

(1) Following Arraignment. Unless a defendant has filed the Waiver, within twenty-eight (28) days of arraignment—or within fourteen (14) days of receipt by the government of a written statement by the defendant that no Waiver will be filed—the government must produce to the defendant:

. . . (2) Exculpatory Information. The timing and substance of the disclosure of exculpatory evidence is specifically provided in L.R. 116.2.

RULE 116.2 DISCLOSURE OF EXCULPATORY EVIDENCE

(A) Definition. Exculpatory information includes, but may not be limited to, all information that is material and favorable to the accused because it tends to:

(1) Cast doubt on defendant's guilt as to any essential element in any count in the indictment or information;

(2) Cast doubt on the admissibility of evidence that the government anticipates offering in its case-in-chief, that might be subject to a motion to suppress or exclude, which would, if allowed, be appealable pursuant to *18 U.S.C. § 3731*;

(3) Cast doubt on the credibility or accuracy of any evidence that the government anticipates offering in its case-in-chief; or

(4) Diminish the degree of the defendant's culpability or the defendant's Offense Level under the United States Sentencing Guidelines.

(B) Timing of Disclosure by the Government. Unless the defendant has filed the Waiver or the government invokes the declination procedure under Rule 116.6, the government must produce to that defendant exculpatory information in accordance with the following schedule:

(1) Within the time period designated in L.R. 116.1(C)(1):

(a) Information that would tend directly to negate the defendant's guilt concerning any count in the indictment or information.

(b) Information that would cast doubt on the admissibility of evidence that the government anticipates offering in its case-in-chief and that could be subject to a motion to suppress or exclude, which would, if allowed, be appealable under *18 U.S.C. § 3731.*

(c) A statement whether any promise, reward, or inducement has been given to any witness whom the government anticipates calling in its case-in-chief, identifying by name each such witness and each promise, reward, or inducement, and a copy of any promise, reward, or inducement reduced to writing.

(d) A copy of any criminal record of any witness identified by name whom the government anticipates calling in its case-in-chief.

(e) A written description of any criminal cases pending against any witness identified by name whom the government anticipates calling in its case-in-chief.

(f) A written description of the failure of any percipient witness identified by name to make a positive identification of a defendant, if any identification procedure has been held with such a witness with respect to the crime at issue.

(2) Not later than twenty-one (21) days before the trial date established by the judge who will preside:

(a) Any information that tends to cast doubt on the credibility or accuracy of any witness whom or evidence that the government anticipates calling or offering in its case-in-chief.

(b) Any inconsistent statement, or a description of such a statement, made orally or in writing by any witness whom the government anticipates calling in its case-in-chief, regarding the alleged criminal conduct of the defendant.

(c) Any statement or a description of such a statement, made orally or in writing by any person, that is inconsistent with any statement made orally or in writing by any witness the government anticipates calling in its case-in-chief, regarding the alleged criminal conduct of the defendant.

(d) Information reflecting bias or prejudice against the defendant by any witness whom the government anticipates calling in its case-in-chief.

(e) A written description of any prosecutable federal offense known by the government to have been committed by any witness whom the government anticipates calling in its case-in-chief.

(f) A written description of any conduct that may be admissible under *Fed. R. Evid. 608(b)* known by the government to have been committed by a witness whom the government anticipates calling in its case-in-chief.

(g) Information known to the government of any mental or physical impairment of any witness whom the government anticipates calling in its case-in-chief, that may cast doubt on the ability of that witness to testify accurately or truthfully at trial as to any relevant event.

(3) No later than the close of the defendant's case: Exculpatory information regarding any witness or evidence that the government intends to offer in rebuttal.

(4) Before any plea or to the submission by the defendant of any objections to the Pre-Sentence Report, whichever first occurs: A written summary of any information in the government's possession that tends to diminish the degree of the defendant's culpability or the defendant's Offense Level under the United States Sentencing Guidelines.

(5) If an item of exculpatory information can reasonably be deemed to fall into more than one of the foregoing categories, it shall be deemed for purposes of determining when it must be produced to fall into the category which requires the earliest production.

Eastern District of Michigan

STANDING ORDER FOR DISCOVERY AND INSPECTION AND FIXING MOTION CUT-OFF DATE IN CRIMINAL CASES

. . . (b) The government shall permit defense counsel to inspect, copy or photocopy any exculpatory evidence within the meaning of *Brady v. Maryland* and *U.S. v. Agurs*.

Western District of Michigan

STANDING ORDER OF DISCOVERY IN CRIMINAL CASES

. . . D. The government shall reveal to the defendant and permit inspection and copying all information and material known to the government which may be favorable to the defendant on the issues of guilt or punishment within the scope of *Brady v. Maryland* and *U.S. v. Agurs*.

Western District of Missouri

SCHEDULING AND TRIAL ORDER

. . . VI. Evidence Favorable to the Defense
 . . . A. *Brady* Evidence
The government is directed to disclose all evidence favorable to the defendant within the meaning of *Brady v. Maryland*.

District of Nebraska

ORDER FOR PROGRESSION OF A CRIMINAL CASE

Upon arraignment of Defendant this date and the entry of plea of not guilty,
IT IS ORDERED:
. . . the United States Attorney shall disclose *Brady v. Maryland* (and its progeny) material as soon as practicable.

District of New Hampshire

Rule 16.1. ROUTINE DISCOVERY

The parties shall disclose the following information without waiting for a demand from the opposing party.
. . . (c) Exculpatory and Impeachment Material.

The government shall disclose any evidence material to issues of guilt or punishment within the meaning of *Brady v. Maryland, 373 U.S. 83 (1963),* and related cases, and any impeachment material as defined in *Giglio v. United States, 405 U.S. 150 (1972),* and related cases, at least twenty (20) days before trial. For good cause shown, the government may seek approval to disclose said material at a later time.

District of New Jersey

ORDER FOR DISCOVERY AND INSPECTION

. . . 1. *CONFERENCE*. Within ten (10) days from the date hereof, the United States Attorney or one of his assistants and the defendant's attorney shall meet and confer, and the government shall:

(f) Permit defendant's attorney to inspect, copy or photograph any exculpatory evidence within the purview of *Brady v. Maryland*.

District of New Mexico

RULE 16.1 DISCOVERY OF EVIDENCE

The Parties will comply with the Standard Discovery Order. A copy of the Order is attached to these Rules.

STANDARD DISCOVERY ORDER

. . . 6. DISCLOSURE OF *BRADY, GIGLIO* AND JENCKS ACT MATERIALS. The government shall make available to the Defendant by the time required by applicable law all material for which discovery is mandated by *Brady v. Mary-*

land,* 373 U.S. 83 (1963), by *Giglio v. United States*, 405 U.S. 150 (1972), and by the Jencks Act, 18 U.S.C. § 3500, and Rules 12(i) and 26.2.

Northern District of New York

14.1 DISCOVERY

. . . (b) Fourteen (14) days after arraignment, or on a date that the Court otherwise sets for good cause shown, the government shall make available for inspection and copying to the defendant the following:

    1. *Brady* Material. All information and material that the government knows that may be favorable to the defendant on the issues of guilt or punishment, within the scope of *Brady v. Maryland*, 373 U.S. 83 (1963).

Eastern District of North Carolina

Rule 16.1. MOTIONS RELATING TO DISCOVERY AND INSPECTION

. . . At the pre-trial conference and upon the request of counsel for the defendant, the government shall permit counsel for the defendant:

. . . (6) to inspect, copy or photograph any exculpatory evidence.

District of North Dakota

PRETRIAL ORDER (CRIMINAL)

. . . II. DISCOVERY: The following discovery rules shall apply:

    . . . d) The Government shall disclose to the Defendant any exculpatory material discoverable under *Brady v. Maryland*, 373 U.S. 83 (1963) and its progeny.

District of the Northern Mariana Islands

LCrR 17.1.1—PRETRIAL CONFERENCE

. . . c. Production of evidence favorable to the defendant on the issue of guilt or punishment as required by *Brady v. Maryland*, 373 U.S. 83 (1963), and related authorities . . .

Western District of Oklahoma

LCrR16.1 DISCOVERY CONFERENCE

(b) Joint Statement. Within three (3) days following completion of the required discovery conference, the parties shall file with the Court Clerk a joint statement memorializing the discovery conference.

JOINT DISCOVERY STATEMENT

. . . 5. The fact of disclosure of all materials favorable to the defendant or the absence thereof within the meaning of *Brady v. Maryland* and related cases:

Counsel for plaintiff expressly acknowledges continuing responsibility to disclose any material favorable to defendant within the meaning of *Brady* that becomes known to the Government during the course of these proceedings.

Western District of Pennsylvania

Rule 16.1. DISCOVERY AND INSPECTION

. . . F. Within five (5) days after the arraignment, the United States attorney shall permit the defendant or defendant's attorney to inspect, copy or photocopy any evidence favorable to the defendant.

Eastern District of Tennessee

DISCOVERY AND SCHEDULING ORDER

. . . The government shall reveal to the defendant and permit inspection and copying of all information and material known to the government which may be favorable to the defendant on the issues of guilt or punishment within the scope of *Brady v. Maryland*, 373 U.S. 83 (1963), *United States v. Agurs*, 427 U.S. 97 (1976) (exculpatory evidence), and *United States v. Bagley*, 473 U.S. 667 (1985) (impeachment evidence). Timing of such disclosure is governed by *United States v. Presser*, 844 F.2d 1275 (6th Cir. 1988).

Middle District of Tennessee

LcrR16.01. DISCOVERY AND INSPECTION

. . . d. The government shall reveal to the defendant and permit inspection and copying of all information and material known to the government which may be favorable to the defendant on the issues of guilt or punishment within the scope of *Brady v. Maryland, 373 U.S. 83, 83 S.Ct. 1194, 10 L.Ed.2d 215 (1963)*, and *United States v. Agurs, 427 U.S. 97, 96 S.Ct. 2392, 49 L.Ed.2d 342 (1976)*.

Western District of Texas

Rule CR-16 DISCOVERY AND INSPECTION

(a) Discovery Conference and Agreement.

(1) The parties need not make standard discovery requests, motions, or responses if, not later than the deadline for filing pretrial motions (or as otherwise authorized by the court), they confer, attempt to agree on procedures for pretrial discovery, and sign and file a copy of the Disclosure Agreement Checklist appended to this rule.

PARTIES' DISCLOSURE AGREEMENT CHECKLIST

Disclosed   Will Disclose/Refuse to   Not   Comments

. . . Rule 16 material:

. . . Exculpatory material . . .
(*Brady*)

District of Vermont

Rule 16.1. DISCOVERY

. . . (a) Disclosure from Government. Within 14 days of arraignment, or on a date otherwise set by the court for good cause shown, the government will make available to the defendant for inspection and copying the following:

. . . (2) *Brady* Material. All information and material known to the government which may be favorable to the defendant on the issues of guilt or punishment, within the scope of *Brady v. Maryland, 373 U.S. 83 (1963)*.

CRIMINAL PRETRIAL ORDER

. . . II. DISCOVERY:

A. Discovery from Government. Within 14 days of arraignment, or on a date otherwise set by the Court for good cause shown, the government shall make available to the defendant for inspection and copying the following:

. . . 2. *Brady* Material. All information and material known to the government which may be favorable to the defendant on the issues of guilt or punishment, within the scope of *Brady v. Maryland, 373 U.S. 83 (1963)*.

Western District of Washington

Rule 16. DISCOVERY AND INSPECTION

. . . (1) Discovery from the government. At the discovery conference the attorney for the government shall comply with the government's obligations under Rule 16 including, but not limited to, the following:

. . . (K) Advise the attorney for the defendant and provide, if requested, evidence favorable to the defendant and material to the defendant's guilt or punishment to which he is entitled pursuant to *Brady v. Maryland* and *United States v. Agurs* . . .

Northern District of West Virginia

LR Cr P 16.05. EXCULPATORY EVIDENCE

Exculpatory evidence as defined in *Brady v. Maryland*, 373 U.S. 83, 83 S. Ct. 1194, 10 L.Ed.2d 215 (1963), as amplified by *United States v. Bagley*, 473 U.S. 667, 105 S. Ct. 3375, 87 L.Ed.2d 481 (1985), shall be disclosed at the time the disclosures described in LR Cr P 16.01 are made. Additional *Brady* material not known to the government at the time of disclosure of other discovery material, as described above, shall be disclosed immediately in writing setting forth the material in detail.

Southern District of West Virginia

ARRAIGNMENT ORDER AND STANDARD DISCOVERY REQUESTS

. . . 1. On Behalf of the Defendant, the Government Is Requested to: (defense counsel must initial all applicable sections)

. . . H. Disclose to defendant all evidence favorable to defendant, including impeachment evidence, and allow defendant to inspect, copy or photograph such evidence.

Eastern District of Wisconsin

Criminal L.R. 16.1 OPEN FILE POLICY

. . . (b) As defined by the United States Attorney's Office, "open file policy" means disclosure without defense motion of all information and materials listed in Fed.R.Crim.P. 16(a)(1)(A), (B), and (D); upon defense request, material listed in Fed.R.Crim.P. 16(a)(1)(C); material disclosable under *18 U.S.C. § 3500* other than grand jury transcripts; reports of interviews with witnesses the government intends to call in its case-in-chief relating to the subject matter of the testimony of the witness; relevant substantive investigative reports; and all exculpatory material. The government must retain the authority to redact from open file material anything (i) that is not exculpatory and (ii) that the government reasonably believes is not relevant to the prosecution, or would jeopardize the safety of a person other than the defendant, or would jeopardize an ongoing criminal investigation. The defendant retains the right to challenge such redactions by motion to the Court.

Appendix C

Sample of Individual Judge Orders Addressing *Brady* Disclosures

---

District of the District of Columbia
(Judge Walton)

GENERAL ORDER GOVERNING CRIMINAL CASES

... (7)   **DISCOVERY MOTIONS:**

The court requires counsel to confer and attempt to resolve all discovery disputes informally. If counsel must file a motion pertaining to a discovery matter, the motion **must** comply with **Local Criminal Rule 16.1**.

(a) **BRADY/GIGLIO EVIDENCE:** If defense counsel believes that the defense is entitled to pretrial disclosure of *Brady/Giglio* material and the government has not complied with its obligations to produce such material, defense counsel should immediately file a motion requesting that the court order the production of such evidence. In the event a motion for the production of *Brady/Giglio* evidence is filed, the court will forthwith convene a hearing during which it will ascertain whether such evidence exists, and if so, when it must be produced. Failure to file a motion despite defense counsel's belief that the defense is in need of pretrial disclosure of *Brady/Giglio* evidence to effectively prepare and present a defendant's case, will weigh heavily against a request by a defendant for a continuance on the eve of trial based on the untimely disclosure of *Brady/Giglio* evidence by the government. In any event, the government is required to provide to the defendant *Brady/Giglio* evidence "at such a time as to allow the defense to use the favorable material effectively in the *preparation and presentation of its case* . . ." United States v. Pollock, 534 F.2d at 973 (emphasis added). If the government believes that such disclosure should not occur sufficiently in advance of a defendant's opening statement so as to afford defense counsel the opportunity to incorporate the *Brady/Giglio* material into the defendant's opening statement, government counsel must advise the Court of the reason(s) for the non-disclosure so the Court can determine when disclosure shall occur. The timing of the disclosure in such situations will be determined by the Court based on the individual circumstances of the particular case.

Middle District of Florida
(Judge Bucklew)

PRETRIAL DISCOVERY ORDER AND NOTICE OF TRIAL AND STATUS CONFERENCE

. . . II. At an appropriate time and after considering any written requests made to the Government by defendant(s):

    A. The Government shall reveal to the defendant and permit inspection and copying of all information and material known to the Government which may be favorable to the defendant on the issue of guilt or punishment within the scope of *Brady v. Maryland*, 373 U.S. 83 (1963), and *United States v. Agurs*, 427 U.S. 97 (1976).

Middle District of Florida
(Judge Corrigan)

JUDGE CORRIGAN'S STANDING ORDER PERTAINING TO DISCOVERY, MOTIONS, HEARINGS, CONFERENCES AND TRIAL

. . . E. Not later than five (5) working days before trial, the Government shall reveal to the defendant(s) all information and material known to the Government which may be favorable to the defendant(s) on the issue of guilt or punishment within the scope of *Brady v. Maryland*, 373 U.S. 83 (1963).

Northern District of Iowa
(Judge Bennett)

ORDER SETTING JURY TRIAL IN CRIMINAL CASES and STIPULATED DISCOVERY ORDER

. . . ***XVII. STIPULATED DISCOVERY ORDER:*** At the time of arraignment, the following discovery obligations were agreed to by the parties, and the Court **ORDERS** compliance with the same.

    A. The United States will include in its open discovery file or otherwise make available law enforcement reports (excluding evaluative material of matters such as possible defenses and legal strategies), grand jury testimony, and evidence or existing summaries of evidence in the custody of the United States Attorney's Office, which provide the basis for the case against the defendant. The file will include Rule 16, *Brady*, and Jencks Act materials of which the United States Attorney's Office is aware and which said Office possesses. Should the defendant become aware of any *Brady* material not contained in the open discovery file, the defendant will notify the United States Attorney's Office of such materials in order that the information may be obtained.

B. The United States may redact or withhold information from the open discovery file for security concerns or to protect an ongoing investigation. This does not preclude the defendant from requesting *in camera* review of such material by the court, upon proper showing, in order to determine whether or not it should be disclosed in accordance with Federal Rule of Criminal Procedure 16. Where the United States withholds information from the open discovery file, notice of the withholding along with a general description of the type of material withheld will be included in the open discovery file. The open discovery file will also not contain evidence which the United States has decided to use for impeachment of defense witnesses or rebuttal evidence. It will not include evaluative material of matters such as possible defenses and legal strategies or other attorney work product. The United States is authorized to disclose any defendant's tax information in its file to co-defendants for use consistent with this Order.

C. The information in the United States's discovery file may only be used for the limited purpose of discovery and in connection with the above-captioned federal criminal case now pending against the defendant. The information provided in discovery shall not be disclosed to or used by any person other than that defendant and his or her counsel, and may not be used or disclosed in any proceeding not part of the pending criminal case. This paragraph does not prohibit the sharing of information by co-defendants in this federal criminal case between or among counsel who are subject to this Order. No information obtained through discovery shall be shared with other defendants or their counsel who are not subject to this Order except through motion pleading, or the offer of trial and sentencing exhibits.

District of Puerto Rico
(Judge Cerezo)

SCHEDULING ORDER

... 1. Automatic discovery by the government of the following material and information in its possession, custody or control, the existence of which is known, or by the exercise of due diligence may become known, to the attorney for the government.

Within the term provided above, except where otherwise provided, the government shall disclose and allow the defendant to inspect, copy and photograph:

> (F) all information and material known to the government which may be favorable to the defendant on the issues of guilt or punishment within the scope of *Brady v. Maryland*, 373 U.S. 83 (1963) and *Kyles v. Whitley*, 115 S.Ct. 1555 (1995).

Appendix D

U.S. Attorney's Manual, Section 9-5.000, Issues Related to Trials and Other Court Proceedings

9-5.000
ISSUES RELATED TO TRIALS AND OTHER COURT PROCEEDINGS

9-5.001	Policy Regarding Disclosure of Exculpatory and Impeachment Information
9-5.100	Policy Regarding the Disclosure to Prosecutors of Potential Impeachment Information Concerning Law Enforcement Agency Witnesses ("Giglio Policy")
9-5.110	Testimony of FBI Laboratory Examiners
9-5.150	Authorization to Close Judicial Proceedings to Members of the Press and Public

9-5.001   Policy Regarding Disclosure of Exculpatory and Impeachment Information

A. **Purpose.** Consistent with applicable federal statutes, rules, and case law, the policy set forth here is intended to promote regularity in disclosure practices, through the reasoned and guided exercise of prosecutorial judgment and discretion by attorneys for the government, with respect to the government's obligation both to disclose exculpatory and impeachment information to criminal defendants and to seek a just result in every case. The policy is intended to ensure timely disclosure of an appropriate scope of exculpatory and impeachment information so as to ensure that trials are fair. The policy, however, recognizes that other interests, such as witness security and national security, are also critically important, *see* USAM § 9-21.000, and that if disclosure prior to trial might jeopardize these interests, disclosure may be delayed or restricted (*e.g.* pursuant to the Classified Information Procedures Act). This policy is not a substitute for researching the legal issues that may arise in an individual case. Additionally, this policy does not alter or supersede the policy that requires prosecutors to disclose "substantial evidence that directly negates the guilt of a subject of the investigation" to the grand jury before seeking an indictment, *see* USAM § 9-11.233.

B. **Constitutional obligation to ensure a fair trial and disclose material exculpatory and impeachment evidence.** Government disclosure of material exculpatory and impeachment evidence is part of the constitutional guarantee to a fair trial. *Brady v. Maryland*, 373 U.S. 83, 87 (1963); *Giglio v. United States*, 405 U.S. 150, 154 (1972). The law requires the disclosure of exculpatory and impeachment evidence when such evidence is material to guilt or punishment. *Brady*, 373 U.S. at 87; *Giglio*, 405 U.S. at 154. Because they are Constitutional obligations, *Brady* and *Giglio* evidence must be disclosed regardless of whether the defendant makes a request for exculpatory or impeachment evidence. *Kyles v. Whitley*, 514 U.S. 419, 432-33 (1995). Neither the Constitution nor this policy, however, creates a general discovery right for trial preparation or plea negotiations. *U.S. v. Ruiz*, 536 U.S. 622, 629 (2002); *Weatherford v. Bursey*, 429 U.S. 545, 559 (1977).

  1. **Materiality and Admissibility.** Exculpatory and impeachment evidence is material to a finding of guilt – and thus the Constitution requires disclosure – when there is a reasonable probability that effective use of the evidence will result in an acquittal. *United States v. Bagley*, 475 U.S. 667, 676 (1985). Recognizing that it is sometimes difficult to assess the materiality of evidence before trial, prosecutors generally must take a broad view of materiality and err on the side of disclosing exculpatory and impeaching evidence. *Kyles*, 514 U.S. at 439. While ordinarily, evidence that would not be admissible at trial need not be disclosed, this policy encourages prosecutors to err on the side of disclosure if admissibility is a close question.

  2. **The prosecution team.** It is the obligation of federal prosecutors, in preparing for trial, to seek all exculpatory and impeachment information from all the members of the prosecution team. Members of the prosecution team include federal, state, and local law enforcement officers and other government officials participating in the investigation and prosecution of the criminal case against the defendant. *Kyles*, 514 U.S. at 437.

C. **Disclosure of exculpatory and impeachment information beyond that which is constitutionally and legally required.** Department policy recognizes that a fair trial will often include examination of relevant exculpatory or impeachment information that is significantly probative of the issues before the court but that may not, on its own, result in an acquittal or, as is often colloquially expressed, make the difference between guilt and innocence. As a result, this policy requires disclosure by prosecutors of information beyond that which is "material" to guilt as articulated in *Kyles v. Whitley*, 514 U.S. 419 (1995), and *Strickler v. Greene*, 527 U.S. 263, 280-81 (1999). The policy recognizes, however, that a trial should not involve the consideration of information which is irrelevant or not significantly probative of the issues before the court and should not involve spurious issues or arguments which serve to divert the trial process from examining the genuine issues. Information that goes only to such matters does not advance the purpose of a trial and thus is not subject to disclosure.

1. **Additional exculpatory information that must be disclosed.** A prosecutor must disclose information that is inconsistent with any element of any crime charged against the defendant or that establishes a recognized affirmative defense, regardless of whether the prosecutor believes such information will make the difference between conviction and acquittal of the defendant for a charged crime.

2. **Additional impeachment information that must be disclosed.** A prosecutor must disclose information that either casts a substantial doubt upon the accuracy of any evidence – including but not limited to witness testimony – the prosecutor intends to rely on to prove an element of any crime charged, or might have a significant bearing on the admissibility of prosecution evidence. This information must be disclosed regardless of whether it is likely to make the difference between conviction and acquittal of the defendant for a charged crime.

3. **Information.** Unlike the requirements of *Brady* and its progeny, which focus on evidence, the disclosure requirement of this section applies to information regardless of whether the information subject to disclosure would itself constitute admissible evidence.

4. **Cumulative impact of items of information.** While items of information viewed in isolation may not reasonably be seen as meeting the standards outlined in paragraphs 1 and 2 above, several items together can have such an effect. If this is the case, all such items must be disclosed.

D. **Timing of disclosure.** Due process requires that disclosure of exculpatory and impeachment evidence material to guilt or innocence be made in sufficient time to permit the defendant to make effective use of that information at trial. *See, e.g. Weatherford v. Bursey*, 429 U.S. 545, 559 (1997); *United States v. Farley*, 2 F.3d 645, 654 (6th Cir. 1993). In most cases, the disclosures required by the Constitution and this policy will be made in advance of trial.

    1. **Exculpatory information.** Exculpatory information must be disclosed reasonably promptly after it is discovered. This policy recognizes that exculpatory information that includes classified or otherwise sensitive national security material may require certain protective measures that may cause disclosure to be delayed or restricted (*e.g.* pursuant to the Classified Information Procedures Act).

    2. **Impeachment information.** Impeachment information, which depends on the prosecutor's decision on who is or may be called as a government witness, will typically be disclosed at a reasonable time before trial to allow the trial to proceed efficiently. In some cases, however, a prosecutor may have to balance the goals of early disclosure against other significant interests – such as witness security and national security – and may conclude that it is not appropriate to provide early disclosure. In such cases, required disclosures may be made at a time and in a manner consistent with the policy embodied in the Jencks Act, 18 U.S.C. § 3500.

    3. **Exculpatory or impeachment information casting doubt upon sentencing factors.** Exculpatory and impeachment information that casts doubt upon proof of an aggravating factor at sentencing, but that does not relate to proof of guilt, must be disclosed no later than the court's initial presentence investigation.

    4. **Supervisory approval and notice to the defendant.** A prosecutor must obtain supervisory approval not to disclose impeachment information before trial or not to disclose exculpatory information reasonably promptly because of its classified nature. Upon such approval, notice must be provided to the defendant of the time and manner by which disclosure of the exculpatory or impeachment information will be made.

E. **Comment.** This policy establishes guidelines for the exercise of judgment and discretion by attorneys for the government in determining what information to disclose to a criminal defendant pursuant to the government's disclosure obligation as set out in *Brady v. Maryland* and *Giglio v. United States* and its obligation to seek justice in every case. As the

Supreme Court has explained, disclosure is required when evidence in the possession of the prosecutor or prosecution team is material to guilt, innocence or punishment. This policy encourages prosecutors to err on the side of disclosure in close questions of materiality and identifies standards that favor greater disclosure in advance of trial through the production of exculpatory information that is inconsistent with any element of any charged crime and impeachment information that casts a substantial doubt upon either the accuracy of any evidence the government intends to rely on to prove an element of any charged crime or that might have a significant bearing on the admissibility of prosecution evidence. Under this policy, the government's disclosure will exceed its constitutional obligations. This expanded disclosure policy, however, does not create a general right of discovery in criminal cases. Nor does it provide defendants with any additional rights or remedies. Where it is unclear whether evidence or information should be disclosed, prosecutors are encouraged to reveal such information to defendants or to the court for inspection *in camera* and, where applicable, seek a protective order from the Court. By doing so, prosecutors will ensure confidence in fair trials and verdicts. Prosecutors are also encouraged to undertake periodic training concerning the government's disclosure obligation and the emerging case law surrounding that obligation.

Appendix E

State Court Policies for the Treatment of *Brady* Material[*]

State Court Policies for the Treatment of *Brady* Material

This section describes state court statutes, rules, orders, and procedures that codify the *Brady* rule or incorporate specific aspects of it, define *Brady* material and/or set the timing and conditions for its disclosure, impose any due diligence obligations on the government, and specify sanctions for the government's failure to comply with such disclosure procedures.

A. Research Methods

We identified within all fifty states and the District of Columbia the relevant statewide legal authority governing prosecutorial disclosure of information favorable to the defendant. We searched relevant databases in Westlaw and LEXIS, including state statutes, criminal procedure rules, state court rules governing criminal discovery, state constitutions, state court opinions, and state rules on professional conduct. For most states, we were able to locate a relevant state rule, order, or other legal authority when we used the following search terms in various combinations:

- "exculpatory evidence";
- "favorable evidence";
- "*Brady* material";
- "prosecution disclosure"; and
- "suppression of evidence."

If we were unable to locate a rule for a state, we reviewed state court opinions to determine if case law addressed or clarified the legal obligation regarding prosecutorial disclosure of information favorable to the defendant.

Our analyses and conclusions are based on our interpretation of the relevant authorities that we identified. We looked for relevant legal authority that contained clear and unequivocal language regarding the duty of the prosecutor to disclose information to the defense. Where we could not identify authority with clear language regarding the prosecution's disclosure obligation, we erred on the side of caution and noted the absence of a clear authority regarding the duty to disclose.

---

[*] For a summary of state court policies, see page 61.

B. Governing Rules, Orders, and Procedures

All fifty states and the District of Columbia address the prosecutor's obligation to disclose information favorable to the defendant. Table 3 shows the sources of the relevant authority.

Table 3. Sources of Authority for Prosecutor's Obligation to Disclose Evidence Favorable to the Defendant

Authorities[70]	Number of States	States
Rules of Criminal Procedure or general court rules	35	Ala., Alaska, Ariz., Ark., Colo., Del., D.C., Fla., Idaho, Ill., Ind., Iowa, Ky., Me., Md., Mass., Mich., Minn., Miss., Mo., N.H., N.J., N.M., N.D., Ohio, Pa., R.I., S.C., Tenn., Utah, Vt., Va., Wash., W. Va., Wyo.
General statutes	14	Conn., Ga., Kan., La., Mont., Neb., Nev., N.Y., N.C., Okla., Or., S.D., Tex., Wis.
Penal code	2	Cal., Haw.

Some state supreme courts have found prosecutors' suppression of exculpatory evidence to violate the due process clauses of their constitutions. For example, in *State v. Hatfield,* the West Virginia Supreme Court held that "[a] prosecution that withholds evidence which if made available would tend to exculpate an accused by creating a reasonable doubt as to his guilt violates due process of law under Article III, Section 14 of the West Virginia Constitution."[71] Another state, Nevada, explicitly notes in its criminal discovery procedure statute that "[t]he provisions of this section are not intended to affect any obligation placed upon the prosecuting attorney by the constitution of this state . . . to disclose exculpatory evidence to the defendant."[72]

C. Definition of *Brady* Material

In thirty-three of the fifty-one jurisdictions, we found rules or procedures that codify the *Brady* rule. There are differences in the *Brady*-related definitions of materials covered.

---

70. We identified several states that address the favorable evidence disclosure obligation in more than one source, e.g., in a statute as well as in a rule. We charted only the highest authority.
71. 286 S.E.2d 402, 411 (W. Va. 1982).
72. Nev. Rev. Stat. § 174.235(3) (2004).

1. Evidence favorable to the defendant

Although there is some variation in the specific language used to define *Brady* material,[73] twenty-three states[74] have adopted language generally resembling the following: "any material or information which tends to negate the guilt of the accused as to the offense charged or would tend to reduce the accused's punishment therefor."[75]

2. Exculpatory evidence or material

Ten other states[76] expressly list exculpatory material as items of information that prosecutors are required to disclose. These states describe exculpatory material in two ways: as "exculpatory evidence"[77] or as "exculpatory material."[78]

The remaining states do not appear to have any express language regarding *Brady* material, but case law in several of those states discusses the *Brady* obligation. For example, in *Potts v. State*, the Georgia Supreme Court held that the "[d]efendant . . . has the burden of showing that the evidence withheld from him so impaired his defense that he was denied a fair trial within the meaning of the *Brady* Rule."[79] The Supreme Court of Wyoming noted that although "[t]here is no general constitutional right to discovery in a criminal case. . . . [s]uppression of evidence favorable to an accused upon request violates due process where the evidence is material to guilt."[80] Other state courts have similarly invoked the *Brady* rule in their decisions.[81]

No state procedure expressly refers to impeaching evidence as material subject to disclosure requirements, but three states specify that prosecutors must turn over any information required to be produced under the Due Process Clause of

---

73. *See, e.g.,* Me. R. Crim. P. 16(a)(1)(C) ("any matter or information known to the attorney for the state which may not be known to the defendant and which tends to create a reasonable doubt of the defendant's guilt as to the offense charged").

74. Ala., Ariz., Ark., Colo., Fla., Haw., Idaho, Ill., Ky., La., Me., Md., Minn., Mo., Mont., N.J., N.M., Ohio, Okla., Pa., Tex., Utah, and Wash.

75. Idaho Crim. R. 16(a).

76. Cal., Conn., Mass., Mich., Miss., Nev., N.H., Tenn., Vt., Wis.

77. *See, e.g.,* Nev. Rev. Stat. § 174.235(3).

78. *See, e.g.,* Cal. Penal Code § 1054.1(e).

79. 243 S.E.2d 510, 517 (Ga. 1978) (citation omitted).

80. Dodge v. State, 562 P.2d 303, 307 (Wyo. 1977) (citations omitted).

81. Bui v. State, 717 So. 2d 6, 27 (Ala. Crim. App. 1997) ("In order to prove a *Brady* violation, a defendant must show (1) that the prosecution suppressed evidence, (2) that the evidence was of a character favorable to his defense, and (3) that the evidence was material." (citation omitted)); O'Neil v. State, 691 A.2d 50, 54 (Del. 1997) ("[T]he [prosecution's] obligation to disclose exculpatory information is triggered by the defendant's request pursuant to Super. Ct. Crim. Rule 16 and is not limited to trial proceedings."); Lomax v. Commonwealth, 319 S.E.2d 763, 766 (Va. 1984) ("[T]he Commonwealth has a duty to disclose the [*Brady*] materials in sufficient time to afford an accused an opportunity to assess and develop the evidence for trial.").

the U.S. Constitution.[82] Two states require disclosure pursuant to the *Brady* decision.[83] Despite this lack of express language, however, it appears that any state court opinion that cites the *Brady* rule would include impeachment evidence as material that state prosecutors are constitutionally obliged to produce for defendants.[84]

D. Disclosure Requirements

Five states[85] use the term "favorable" in describing evidence subject to the state disclosure obligation. However, these states limit the clause "evidence favorable to the accused" with a condition that such evidence be "material and relevant to the issue of guilt or punishment."[86]

Although *Brady* used "favorable" in describing the evidence required for prosecutorial disclosure,[87] Rule 16 does not expressly refer to "favorable evidence." The rule permits a defendant in federal criminal cases to receive, upon request, documents and tangible objects within the possession of the government that "*are material to the preparation of the defendant's defense* or are intended for use by the government as evidence in chief at the trial, or were obtained from or belong to the defendant."[88] In describing some of the items of evidence subject to the criminal discovery right, twenty-six states use language identical or substantially similar to the italicized language above.[89]

1. *Types of information required to be disclosed*

All of the states[90] require, at a minimum, disclosure of the types of evidence that Rule 16 permits to be disclosed before trial:

---

82. *See, e.g.,* Nev. Rev. Stat. § 174.235(3); N.M. Dist. Ct. R. Cr. P. 5-501(A)(6); N.Y. Consol. Law Serv. Crim. P. Law § 240.20(1)(h).

83. *See, e.g.,* N.H. Super. Ct. R. 98(A)(2)(iv); Tenn. Crim. P. R. 16 (Advisory Commission Comments).

84. *See* United States v. Bagley, 473 U.S. 667, 676 ("Impeachment evidence, as well as exculpatory evidence, falls within the *Brady* rule.").

85. La., N.M., Ohio, Okla., Pa.

86. *See, e.g.,* Pa. R. Crim. P. 573 (B)(1)(a) ("The Commonwealth shall . . . permit the defendant's attorney to inspect and copy or photograph . . . any evidence favorable to the accused that is material either to guilt or to punishment."); La. Code Crim. P. Ann. art. 718 ("[O]n motion of the defendant, the court shall order the district attorney to permit or authorize the defendant to inspect, copy, examine . . . [evidence] favorable to the defendant and which [is] material and relevant to the issue of guilt or punishment.").

87. 373 U.S. at 87 ("[S]uppression by the prosecution of evidence favorable to an accused upon request violates due process where the evidence is material either to guilt or punishment.").

88. Fed. R. Crim. P. 16(a)(1)(C) (emphasis added).

89. Ala., Conn., Del., D.C., Haw., Idaho, Ind., Iowa, Kan., Ky., Miss., Mo., Neb., N.D., Ohio, Pa., S.C., S.D., Tenn., Tex., Utah, Vt., Va., Wash., W. Va., Wyo.

90. Indiana is unique in that it does not contain a separate rule for criminal discovery and relies on civil trial procedural rules to govern criminal trials. *See* Ind. Crim. R. 21 ("The Indiana rules of trial and appellate procedure shall apply to all criminal proceedings."). Therefore, Indiana

- written or recorded statements, admissions, or confessions made by the defendant;
- books, papers, documents, or tangible objects obtained from the defendant;
- reports of experts in connection with results of any physical or mental examinations made of the defendant, and scientific tests or experiments made;
- records of the defendant's prior criminal convictions; and
- written lists of the names and addresses of persons having knowledge of relevant facts who may be called by the state as witnesses at trial.[91]

Some states, however, go beyond this basic list of information and specify other material for disclosure:

- any electronic surveillance of any conversations to which the defendant was a party;[92]
- whether an investigative subpoena has been executed in the case;[93]
- whether the case has involved an informant;[94]
- whether a search warrant has been executed in connection with the case;[95]
- transcripts of grand jury testimony relating to the case given by the defendant, or by a codefendant to be tried jointly;[96]
- police, arrest, and crime or offense reports;[97]
- felony convictions of any material witness whose credibility is likely to be critical to the outcome of the trial;[98]
- all promises, rewards, or inducements made to witnesses the state intends to present at trial;[99]
- DNA laboratory reports revealing a match to the defendant's DNA;[100]
- expert witnesses whom the prosecution will call at the hearing or trial, the subject of their testimony, and any reports they have submitted to the prosecution;[101]

---

does not provide a specific list of evidence subject to criminal discovery. Presumably, however, a criminal defendant in Indiana state court would be entitled to the basic items of evidence listed here.

91. *See, e.g.,* Conn. Gen. Stat. § 54-86(a) (2003); Idaho Crim. Rule 16(a).
92. Mont. Code Ann. § 415-15-322 (2)(a).
93. Mont. Code Ann. § 415-15-322 (2)(b).
94. Mont. Code Ann. § 415-15-322 (2)(c).
95. Ariz. St. RCRP R. 15.1(b)(10).
96. N.Y. Consol. Law Serv. Crim. P. Law § 240.20(1)(b).
97. Colo. Crim. P. Rule 16(a)(I).
98. Cal. Penal Code § 1054.1(d).
99. Mass. Crim. P. R. 14(1)(A)(ix) (as amended, effective Sept. 7, 2004).
100. N.C. Gen. Stat. § 15A-903(g).
101. Wash. Super. Ct. Crim. R. 4.7(a)(2)(ii).

- any information that indicates entrapment of the defendant;[102] and
- "any other evidence specifically identified by the defendant, provided the defendant can additionally establish that its disclosure would be in the interests of justice."[103]

Most states provide that this "favorable" evidence *may* be disclosed to the defendant upon request or at the discretion of the court. Other states require that evidence beyond the scope of *Brady* material *must* be disclosed even without a request or court order.

2. *Mandatory disclosure without request*

Thirteen states[104] require mandatory disclosure of information "favorable" to the defense, regardless of whether the defendant made a specific discovery request for the material. We determined that this disclosure is mandatory because of the use of the phrase "prosecutor *shall* disclose," and the lack of any conditional clause such as "upon defendant's request," or "at the court's discretion." For example, Massachusetts describes as being "mandatory discovery for the defendant" the following items of evidence:

(i) Any written or recorded statements, and the substance of any oral statements, made by the defendant or a co-defendant.

(ii) The grand jury minutes, and the written or recorded statements of a person who has testified before a grand jury.

(iii) Any facts of an exculpatory nature.

(iv) The names, addresses, and dates of birth of the Commonwealth's prospective witnesses other than law enforcement witnesses . . . .

(v) The names and business addresses of prospective law enforcement witnesses.

(vi) Intended expert opinion evidence, other than evidence that pertains to the defendant's criminal responsibility . . . .

(vii) Material and relevant police reports, photographs, tangible objects, all intended exhibits, reports of physical examinations of any person or of scientific tests or experiments, and statements of persons the Commonwealth intends to call as witnesses.

(viii) A summary of identification procedures, and all statements made in the presence of or by an identifying witness that are relevant to the issue of identity or to the fairness or accuracy of the identification procedures.

(ix) Disclosure of all promises, rewards or inducements made to witnesses the Commonwealth intends to present at trial.[105]

---

102. Wash. Super. Ct. Crim. R. 4.7(a)(2)(iii).
103. Pa. R. Crim. P. 573(B)(2)(a)(iv).
104. Alaska, Ariz., Cal., Colo., Fla., Haw., Me., Md., Mass., N.H., N.M., Or., Wash.
105. Mass. Crim. P. Rule 14 (as amended, effective Sept. 7, 2004).

In contrast, Hawaii requires disclosure of evidence favorable to the defendant only if the defendant is charged with a felony.[106] In cases other than felonies, Hawaii permits a state court, at its discretion, to require disclosure of favorable evidence "[u]pon a showing of materiality and if the request is reasonable."[107]

Of the thirteen states that require disclosure of favorable evidence, three distinguish between information that is subject to mandatory disclosure and other evidence that must be specifically requested by the defendant or ordered by the court. Maine requires prosecutors to disclose the following items:

1. Statements obtained as a result of a search and seizure, statements resulting from any confession or admission made by the defendant, statements relating to a lineup or voice identification of the defendant.

2. Any written or recorded statements made by the defendant.

3. Any statement that tends to create a reasonable doubt of the defendant's guilt as to the offense charged.[108]

Maine requires the defendant to make a written request to compel the disclosure of books, papers, documents, tangible objects, reports of experts made in connection with the case, and names and addresses of the witnesses whom the state intends to call in any proceeding.[109]

The other two states that distinguish between items of evidence that are subject to mandatory disclosure are Maryland[110] and Washington.[111]

3. *Disclosure upon request of defendant*

Thirty-eight states[112] require a defendant to request favorable information, sometimes in writing, before the prosecution's obligation to disclose is triggered.

Ten states[113] place an additional condition on the defense:

- the defendant must make "a showing [to the court] that the items sought may be material to the preparation of his defense and that the request is reasonable,"[114] or

- the defendant must show "good cause" for discovery of such information.[115]

---

106. Haw. R. Penal P. 16(a) ("[D]iscovery under this rule may be obtained in and is limited to cases in which the defendant is charged with a felony.").

107. Haw. R. Penal P. 16(d).

108. Me. R. Crim. P. 16(a)(1)(A)–(C).

109. Me. R. Crim. P. 16(b).

110. Md. Rule 4-263.

111. Wash. Super. Ct. Crim. R. 4.7.

112. Ala., Ark., Conn., Del., D.C., Ga., Idaho, Ill., Ind., Iowa, Kan., Ky., La., Mich., Minn., Miss., Mo., Mont., Neb., Nev., N.J., N.Y., N.C., N.D., Ohio, Okla., Pa., R.I., S.C., S.D., Tenn., Tex., Utah, Vt., Va., W. Va., Wis., Wyo.

113. Conn., Idaho, Ind., Minn., Mo., Neb., Pa., Tex., Va., Wash.

114. Conn. Gen. Stat. § 54-86(a).

115. Tex. Code Crim. Proc. art. 39.14 (2004).

It appears that these ten states permit disclosure of certain favorable evidence only at the discretion of the trial court, and only if the court finds that the defendant has met the burden of proof in making the discovery request.

4. *Time requirements for disclosure*

States vary considerably in their time requirements for disclosure of *Brady* material. Some specify a time by which the prosecution must disclose favorable information, while others rely upon undefined terms such as "timely disclosure" or "as soon as practicable." Ten states[116] have established two separate time limits—one for the period within which the defendant must file a discovery request for favorable information and another for the period within which the prosecution must disclose the information.[117]

For a small number of states,[118] we were unable to determine a specific timetable for disclosure of *Brady* material. Nonetheless, it is probable that these states impose a "timely" disclosure requirement that would not prejudice the defendant's right to a fair trial.

a. *Specific time requirement*

Twenty-eight states[119] have mandated specific time limits for prosecutorial disclosure of evidence favorable to the defendant. Table 4 summarizes these time requirements.

Table 4. States with Specific Time Limits for Prosecutorial Disclosure of Evidence Favorable to the Defendant

State	Authority	Time Requirement
Alabama	Ala. R. Cr. P. 16.1	Within 14 days after the request has been filed in court
Arizona	Ariz. St. R. Cr. P. 15.6(c)	Not later than 7 days prior to trial
California	Cal. Penal Code § 1054.7	Not later than 30 days prior to trial
Colorado	Colo. Cr. P. R. 16(b)	Not later than 20 days after filing of charges
Connecticut	Conn. Gen. Stat. § 54-86(c)	Not later than 30 days after defendant pleads not guilty

---

116. D.C., Idaho, Mo., Nev., N.Y., Ohio, Okla., R.I., Va., W. Va.

117. *See, e.g.,* Nev. Rev. Stat. § 174.285 (2004) ("A request . . . may be made only within 30 days after arraignment or at such reasonable later time as the court may permit. . . . A party shall comply with a request made . . . not less than 30 days before trial or at such reasonable later time as the court may permit.").

118. D.C., Iowa, Pa., S.D., Tenn., Tex., Wyo.

119. Ala., Ariz., Cal., Colo., Conn., Del., Fla., Ga., Haw., Idaho, Ind., Kan., Me., Md., Mass., Mich., Minn., Mo., Nev., N.H., N.J., N.M., N.Y., Ohio, Okla., R.I., S.C., Wash.

State	Authority	Time Requirement
Delaware	Del. Super. Ct. Crim. R. 16(d)(3)(B)	Within 20 days after service of discovery request
Florida	Fla. R. Cr. P. 3.220(b)(1)	Within 15 days after service of discovery request
Georgia	Ga. Code Ann. § 17-16-4(a)(1)	Not later than 10 days prior to trial
Hawaii	Haw. R. Penal P. 16(e)(1)	Within 10 calendar days after arraignment and plea of the defendant
Idaho	Idaho Cr. R. 16(e)(1)	Within 14 days after service of discovery request
Indiana	Ind. R. Trial P. 34(B)	Within 30 days after service of discovery request
Kansas	Kan. Stat. Ann. § 22-3212(f)	Within 20 days after arraignment
Maine	Me. R. Crim. P. 16(a)(3)	Within 10 days after arraignment
Maryland	Md. R. 4-263(e)	Within 25 days after appearance of counsel or first appearance of defendant before the court, whichever is earlier
Massachusetts	Mass. Crim. P. R. 14(1)(A)	At or prior to the pretrial conference
Michigan	Mich. Ct. R. 6.201(F)	Within 7 days after service of discovery request
Minnesota	Minn. R. Crim. P. 9.03; Minn. Bd. of Judicial Stand. R. 9(e)	Within 60 days after service of discovery request; by the time of the omnibus hearing
Missouri	Mo. Sup. Ct. R. 25.02	Within 10 days after service of discovery request
Nevada	Nev. Rev. Stat. § 174.285	Not later than 30 days prior to trial
New Hampshire	N.H. Sup. Ct. R. 98(A)(2)	Within 30 days after defendant pleads not guilty
New Jersey	N.J. Ct. R. 3:13-3(b)	Not later than 28 days after the indictment
New Mexico	N.M. R. Crim. P. 5-501(A)	Within 10 days after arraignment
New York	N.Y. Consol. Law Serv. Crim. P. Law § 240.80(3)	Within 15 days after service of discovery request
Ohio	Ohio R. Crim. P. 16(F)	Within 21 days after arraignment or 7 days prior to trial, whichever is earlier
Oklahoma	Okla. Stat. § 2002(D)	Not later than 10 days prior to trial
Rhode Island	R.I. Super. R. Crim. P. 16(g)(1)	Within 15 days after service of discovery request

State	Authority	Time Requirement
South Carolina	S.C. R. Crim. P. 5(a)(3)	Not later than 30 days after service of discovery request
Washington	Wash. Super. Ct. Crim. R. 4.7(a)(1)	No later than the omnibus hearing

b. Nonspecific, descriptive time frame

Eighteen states[120] provide nonspecific, descriptive time requirements for disclosure of *Brady* material. The terms used for these general time frames include the following:

- "timely disclosure";[121]
- "as soon as practicable";[122]
- "a reasonable time in advance of trial date";[123]
- "within a reasonable time";[124]
- "in time for the defendants to make effective use of the evidence";[125]
- "as soon as possible";[126]
- "as soon as reasonably possible";[127] and
- "within a reasonable time before trial."[128]

State case law may provide guidance on whether a particular disclosure has satisfied the "timely" disclosure requirement. In general, however, the state courts have interpreted "timely" or "as soon as possible" to mean that the prosecution must disclose information favorable to the defendant "within a sufficient time for its effective use" by the defendant in preparation for his or her defense.[129] State courts that have ruled on the issue of timing of disclosures have

---

120. Alaska, Ark., Ill., Ky., La., Me., Miss., Mont., Neb., N.C., N.D., Ohio, Or., Utah, Vt., Va., W. Va., Wis.

121. *See, e.g.,* Alaska R. Prof. Conduct 3.8(d); La. R. Prof. Conduct 3.8(d).

122. *See, e.g.,* Ark. R. Crim. P. 17.2(a); Ill. Sup. Ct. R. 412(d).

123. *See, e.g.,* Ky. R. Crim. P. 7.24(4).

124. *See, e.g.,* Me. R. Crim. P. 16(a).

125. *See, e.g.,* State v. Taylor, 472 S.E.2d 596, 607 (N.C. 1996) ("[D]ue process and *Brady* are satisfied by the disclosure of the evidence at trial, so long as disclosure is made in time for the defendants to make effective use of the evidence." (citations omitted)).

126. *See, e.g.,* Vt. R. Crim. P. 16(b).

127. *See, e.g.,* State v. Hager, 342 S.E.2d 281, 284 (W. Va. 1986) ("[W. Va. R. Crim. P.] 16 impliedly sanctions the use of newly discovered evidence at trial, so long as the evidence is disclosed to the defense as soon as reasonably possible.").

128. *See, e.g.,* Wis. Stat. § 971.23(1).

129. State v. Harris, 680 N.W.2d 737, 754–55 (Wis. 2004) ("We hold that in order for evidence to be disclosed 'within a reasonable time before trial' . . . it must be disclosed within a sufficient time for its effective use. Were it otherwise, the State could withhold all *Brady* evidence until

emphasized that any disclosure must not constitute "unfair surprise" to the defendant and must not prejudice the defendant's right to a fair trial.[130]

E. Due Diligence Obligations

By various means each state imposes a continuing duty on the prosecutor to locate and disclose additional favorable information discovered throughout the course of a trial. Delaware's Superior Court Rule 16(c) is typical of the rules in most states with a due diligence obligation:

> If, prior to or during trial, a party discovers additional evidence or material previously requested or ordered, which is subject to discovery or inspection under this rule, such party shall promptly notify the other party or that other party's attorney or the court of the existence of the additional evidence or material.[131]

Beyond this basic duty to supplement discovery of information, five states[132] require prosecutors to certify, in writing, that they have exercised diligent, good faith efforts in locating all favorable information, and that what has been disclosed is accurate and complete to the best of their knowledge or belief. For example, Florida requires the following:

> Every request for discovery or response ... shall be signed by at least 1 attorney of record ... [certifying] that ... to the best of the signer's knowledge, information, or belief formed after a reasonable inquiry it is consistent with these rules and warranted by existing law ....[133]

Similarly, Massachusetts provides:

> When a party has provided all discovery required by this rule or by court order, it shall file with the court a Certificate of Compliance. The certificate shall state that, to the best of its knowledge and after reasonable inquiry, the party has disclosed and made available all items subject to discovery other than reports of experts, and shall identify each item provided.[134]

F. Sanctions for Noncompliance with *Brady* Obligations

All states provide remedies for prosecutorial nondisclosure that follow closely, if not explicitly mirror, Federal Rule of Criminal Procedure 16(d)(2), which states that a "court may order [the prosecution] to permit the discovery or inspection, grant a continuance, or prohibit [the prosecution] from introducing evidence not

---

the day of trial in the hope that the defendant would plead guilty under the false assumption that no such evidence existed.").

130. State v. Golder, 9 P.3d 635 (Mont. 2000) (defendant argued that the timing of the state's formal disclosure of the two witnesses and the nature of their testimony constituted unfair surprise and jeopardized his right to a fair trial as ensured under the Montana Constitution).

131. Del. Super. Ct. R. 16(c).

132. Colo., Fla., Idaho, Mass., N.M.

133. Fla. R. Crim. P. 3.220(n)(3). *See also* Idaho Crim. R. 16(e) (Certificate of Service).

134. Mass. Crim. P. R. 14(a)(1)(E)(3) (as amended, effective Sept. 7, 2004).

disclosed, or it may enter such other order as it deems just under the circumstances."[135]

In addition, eleven states[136] indicate that willful violations of a criminal discovery rule or court order requiring disclosure may subject the prosecution to other sanctions as the court deems appropriate. These sanctions "may include, but are not limited to, contempt proceedings against the attorney . . . as well as the assessment of costs incurred by the opposing party, when appropriate."[137]

At least one state, Idaho, expressly states that failure to comply with the time prescribed for disclosure "shall be grounds for the imposition of sanctions by the court."[138] Other states probably also permit their courts to impose sanctions for failure to meet time requirements, as their rules provide remedies for failure to comply with *any* discovery rules, which can and often do include a time-limits provision.

At least three states[139] allow the court to order a dismissal as a possible sanction for particularly egregious violations of disclosure obligations. For example, Maine's rules state the following:

> If the attorney for the state fails to comply with this rule, the court on motion of the defendant or on its own motion may take appropriate action, which may include, but is not limited to, one or more of the following: requiring the attorney for the state to comply, granting the defendant additional time or a continuance . . . prohibiting the attorney for the state from introducing specified evidence and *dismissing charges with prejudice*.[140]

However, three states[141] regard dismissal to be too severe a sanction for nondisclosure. Louisiana's Code of Criminal Procedure notes that for disclosure violations, their state courts may "enter such other order, *other than dismissal*, as may be appropriate."[142] Similarly, the Supreme Court of Pennsylvania found dismissal to be "too severe" a sanction for failure to disclose *Brady* material, and explained that the discretion of Pennsylvania trial courts "is not unfettered."[143]

---

135. Fed. R. Crim. P. 16(d)(2).
136. Ala., Ark., Fla., Haw., Ill., La., Minn., Mo., N.M., Vt., Wash.
137. Fla. R. Crim. P. 3.220(n)(2).
138. Idaho Crim. R. 16(e)(2).
139. Conn., Me., N.C.
140. Me. R. Crim. P. 16(d) (emphasis added).
141. La., Pa., Tex.
142. La. Code Crim. P. Ann. art. 729.5(A) (emphasis added).
143. Commonwealth v. Burke, 781 A.2d 1136, 1143 (Pa. 2001) ("[O]ur research has revealed [no judicial precedents] that approve or require a discharge as a remedy for a discovery violation. In fact, the precedents cited by the trial court and appellant support the view that the discharge ordered here was too severe . . . . [W]hile it is undoubtedly true that the trial court possesses some discretion in fashioning an appropriate remedy for a *Brady* violation, that discretion is not unfettered.").

Summary of State Court Policies for the Treatment of *Brady* Material

- All fifty states and the District of Columbia have a rule or other type of authority, including statutes, concerning the prosecutor's obligation to disclose information favorable to the defendant.
- Many of the states have enacted rules similar to Federal Rule of Criminal Procedure 16; however, some of these rules and statutes vary in their details. Some states go beyond the scope of Rule 16 and the *Brady* constitutional obligations by explicitly setting time limits on disclosure; other states have adopted Rule 16 almost verbatim, using language like "evidence material to the preparation of the defense" and "evidence favorable to the defendant."
- Most states' rules impose a continuing disclosure obligation, such that if additional evidence is discovered during the trial or after initial disclosure, the defendant must be promptly notified and shown such new evidence.
- A few states have a specific due diligence obligation that requires prosecutors to submit a "certificate of compliance" indicating that they have exercised due diligence in locating favorable evidence and that, to the best of their knowledge and belief, all such information has been disclosed to the defense.
- All of the states authorize sanctions for prosecutors' failure to comply with discovery obligations and other state-court-mandated disclosure requirements. A few states permit a trial court to dismiss charges entirely as a sanction for prosecutorial misconduct, while other states have held dismissal to be too severe a sanction.

The Federal Judicial Center

Board

The Chief Justice of the United States, *Chair*
Judge David O. Carter, U.S. District Court for the Central District of California
Judge Bernice B. Donald, U.S. District Court for the Western District of Tennessee
Judge Terence T. Evans, U.S. Court of Appeals for the Seventh Circuit
Magistrate Judge Karen Klein, U.S. District Court for the District of North Dakota
Judge Philip M. Pro, U.S. District Court for the District of Nevada
Judge Stephen Raslavich, U.S. Bankruptcy Court for the Eastern District of Pennsylvania
Judge Karen J. Williams, U.S. Court of Appeals for the Fourth Circuit
James C. Duff, Director of the Administrative Office of the U.S. Courts

Director

Judge Barbara J. Rothstein

Deputy Director

John S. Cooke

About the Federal Judicial Center

The Federal Judicial Center is the research and education agency of the federal judicial system. It was established by Congress in 1967 (28 U.S.C. §§ 620–629), on the recommendation of the Judicial Conference of the United States.

By statute, the Chief Justice of the United States chairs the Center's Board, which also includes the director of the Administrative Office of the U.S. Courts and seven judges elected by the Judicial Conference.

The organization of the Center reflects its primary statutory mandates. The Education Division plans and produces education and training programs for judges and court staff, including satellite broadcasts, video programs, publications, curriculum packages for in-court training, and Web-based programs and resources. The Research Division examines and evaluates current and alternative federal court practices and policies. This research assists Judicial Conference committees, who request most Center research, in developing policy recommendations. The Center's research also contributes substantially to its educational programs. The two divisions work closely with two units of the Director's Office—the Systems Innovations & Development Office and Communications Policy & Design Office—in using print, broadcast, and online media to deliver education and training and to disseminate the results of Center research. The Federal Judicial History Office helps courts and others study and preserve federal judicial history. The International Judicial Relations Office provides information to judicial and legal officials from foreign countries and assesses how to inform federal judicial personnel of developments in international law and other court systems that may affect their work.